SABRINA REECE

Self Sabotage

Learning Not to Be Your Own Worst Enemy

Copyright © 2026 by SaBrina Reece

All rights reserved. No part of this publication may be reproduced, stored, or transmitted in any form or by any means, electronic, mechanical, photocopying, recording, scanning, or otherwise without written permission from the publisher. It is illegal to copy this book, post it to a website, or distribute it by any other means without permission.

First edition

This book was professionally typeset on Reedsy. Find out more at reedsy.com

Contents

Preface		ii
1	You Are Extraordinary	1
2	The Enemy Inside	4
3	Becoming Your Own Ally	8
4	Get to Know Yourself	12
5	Closing Doors	21
6	Depression	36
7	How to Pray	47
8	You are Worthy	56
9	Demand Happiness	63
10	The Quiet Ways We Undermine Ourselves	71
11	Choosing Yourself: Ending the War Within	77
About the Author		81
Also by SaBrina Reece		82

Preface

This book was written for anyone who has ever felt like the biggest obstacle in their life was not the world around them, but the thoughts they carried within themselves. It is for those who work hard, care deeply, and still find themselves feeling stuck, doubting their worth, or standing in their own way without fully understanding why.

Self-sabotage rarely announces itself loudly. It shows up quietly in the way we speak to ourselves, the risks we avoid, the opportunities we talk ourselves out of, and the dreams we dismiss before they ever have a chance to grow. It lives in the stories we repeat about who we are and what we believe we deserve. Over time, those stories begin to shape our choices, our confidence, and the direction of our lives.

Many of us learned these patterns early. Some of us learned them through trauma, abandonment, criticism, or instability. Others learned them by watching the adults around us speak negatively about themselves or accept lives that did not reflect their true potential. However they began, these patterns are not a reflection of weakness. They are learned behaviors, and anything learned can be unlearned.

This book is not about blaming yourself for where you are. It is about helping you understand how you got here, so you can choose differently moving forward. It is about recognizing the ways negative self-talk, fear-based thinking, and unresolved emotional pain quietly sabotage growth. It is also about reclaiming the power you may not realize you still have.

Throughout these pages, you will be invited to reflect honestly, not harshly. To observe your thoughts without judgment. To notice how often you speak limitations over your own life and how those words shape your reality. This work does not require perfection. It requires awareness, courage, and a willingness to be honest with yourself.

Self-sabotage is not who you are. It is something you learned to survive. And survival is not the same as living.

If you are reading this book, it means some part of you is ready for change. Ready to stop being your own worst enemy and start becoming your own ally. This book is here to walk with you through that shift, offering clarity, understanding, and encouragement along the way.

You do not need to be fixed. You need to be aware.

And awareness is where everything begins.

1

You Are Extraordinary

Whether or not we have come to accept it, we are far more capable than we allow ourselves to be. Like dormant cells within the body, there is no guarantee that each of us will ever fully activate our potential. Many people move through life operating on autopilot, repeating the same routines day after day, believing that survival alone is the goal. But we were placed on this earth to do more than simply eat, sleep, work, and repeat.

Each one of us carries a personal purpose and a unique contribution meant for this world. I truly believe that every human being is born with something valuable to offer. At the same time, I also believe there is no guarantee that we will ever discover or live out that purpose. Not because it is unavailable to us, but because we often sabotage ourselves before we ever give it a chance to emerge.

Life gives us clues. Inspiration shows up quietly and persistently. It appears as recurring thoughts, sudden ideas, creative urges, or dreams that refuse to leave us alone. These moments are not random. They are invitations. Unfortunately, many of us are too busy, too distracted, or too afraid to recognize them.

We talk ourselves out of them. We minimize them. We convince ourselves that we are not qualified, not ready, or not special enough.

That is self-sabotage at its finest.

When inspiration arrives, it deserves attention. Do not assume it will come back. In my experience, ideas are fleeting. They require respect. When something meaningful comes to you, write it down immediately. Do not depend on memory. Memory fades, but written intention remains. I call these moments "Inspiration for Creation." They are a natural ability given to us by God to design and create a meaningful life.

If you ever feel a strong pull toward something you have never done before, listen. That urge may feel unfamiliar or even uncomfortable, but discomfort does not mean danger. Often, it means growth. I believe that many of the ideas we dismiss are actually nudges toward our true destiny. Ignoring them does not make them go away. It simply delays our growth.

We admire people who invent, innovate, and create things that change the world. We read about them. We watch documentaries. We label them as exceptional, gifted, or rare. What we often forget is that the same divine energy that fueled their ideas exists within us as well. Creativity is not reserved for a select few. It is a human trait. Every person has the ability to create something meaningful, whether in their personal life, their community, or the world at large.

The problem is not a lack of ability. The problem is the limits we accept. Many people have spent so much time doubting themselves that they have lost touch with their own power. They shrink their ideas before anyone else ever has the chance to reject them. They talk themselves out of action. They wait for permission that never comes. This is how extraordinary potential gets buried under fear, comparison, and self-doubt.

Self-sabotage often shows up as playing small. It is choosing comfort over curiosity. It is convincing yourself that your ideas are unrealistic or unimportant. It is believing that other people are more deserving of success, creativity, or fulfillment than you are. These beliefs quietly keep people living at an ordinary level, even though they were never created to be ordinary.

I believe the world cannot truly advance until individuals choose to advance internally. That advancement begins by identifying the mental and emotional barriers we have built around ourselves. Fear, insecurity, past failure, and unresolved pain all contribute to self-sabotage. Once you become aware of those barriers, you can begin dismantling them.

This belief is not based on scientific theory. It is based on a lifetime of observation. Most people will live and die having never explored the fullness of who they could have been. Not because they lacked ability, but because they doubted themselves too much to try.

You do not have to be one of them.

Stop living as if you are ordinary when God clearly created you to be extraordinary. Your ideas matter. Your creativity matters. Your contribution matters. The moment you stop standing in your own way is the moment your life begins to expand.

2

The Enemy Inside

Anger is not your friend and it never will be. It is the true enemy inside of you. That is a hard truth to accept, especially in a world that often celebrates loud reactions, dominance, and emotional explosions as strength. For many of us, anger feels powerful. It feels protective. It feels like control. But over time, I learned that anger does not protect us. It isolates us. It does not give us power. It takes it away.

I know anger, I have met it head on personally. As a young woman I was misguided and confused. Alone in the world after my grandmother was taken away from me in a tragic way. I was trying to figure it out. there was no one to teach me about boundaries and how to pull back and take a breath when I felt overwhelmed with emotion. I quickly confused rage with standing up for myself, and that served no positive purpose in my life.

Aside from pushing away people that truly care about you, anger can and will cause severe mental and physical distress. Research supports what many of us feel in our bodies but do not always connect to our emotions. Studies from the American

Psychological Association show that chronic anger is linked to increased risk of heart disease, high blood pressure, stroke, digestive disorders, migraines, and weakened immune function. Anger also significantly increases anxiety and depression over time, even when it feels justified in the moment.

No matter how provoked we feel, we must take a second to take a deep breath and assess the current situation, then proceed with a consciously chosen response, as opposed to one that is reactive and impulsive. Think about everything first. Even if only for a second. That single second can save relationships, careers, reputations, and in some cases, lives.

Take a moment to consider the negative result of an explosive response. Rarely has anything productive ever come from responding out of anger. Anger causes us to hurt those we love and creates unnecessary distance in our relationships with others. It convinces us that being right matters more than being at peace.

I had a very bad temper for many years. We exert so much energy in our confrontations and disagreements with other people. We can get so mad over differences of opinion. When we feel offended or disrespected we feel compelled to "set that person straight," even if doing so requires screaming and exerting extremely negative behavior, which can in turn destroy the relationship. We will declare war on some people and vow never to speak to them again as a punishment. We make enemies and will spend hours having imaginary conversations where we give them a piece of our mind, getting ourselves so upset that we cause permanent wrinkles in our forehead.

These external enemies receive all of our attention thus affecting us physically. It consumes so much of our mind space it can become a huge distraction. It can prevent us from advancing in all areas of our lives. I believe if we declare that same war on our internal enemy, our lives will improve for the better.

The enemy inside is that little voice in your head that tells you that you can't or are incapable of achieving something. I call this inner enemy "mind chatter" and it can lie to us and prevent us from realizing our true potential. This voice has controlled many of us for years. Many people are unaware of this voice. On the contrary, there are others who have recognized the voice, some religious folk even refer to the voice as "the devil' or " The Prince of Lies," yet still have not gained the power to not be affected by the its negative rantings.

Many philosophers refer to the voice as "The Ego". In my opinion, it does not matter what name you call the voice in your head, as long as you realize that everything it tells you is not the truth and you have the power to override all of the negative chatter and replace it with positive self talk.

The internal voice is a product of your subconscious mind. It is fueled by your fears and doubts until you learn to reprogram it. In this book I offer techniques that will assist you in reprogramming and officially declaring war on that negative voice in your head.

Declaring war and effectively winning that war with the enemy of the mind should be the ultimate goal. If the war is won within, all external enemies won't even have the ability to affect us. The true battle is in the mind. Gaining the abilities to control our thinking patterns. Learning to master control of our thoughts will allow us the privilege of only accepting thoughts that serve us well into our mind space and we will develop the ability to cast out negative thoughts and images because they are the true internal enemy.

Maintaining a persistent negative thinking pattern will prove to be more harmful to you than anything you can ever encounter in your life. We must learn the tools needed to declare all out war on anything that prevents us from leading a happy fulfilling life. This is one of the main reasons why I felt compelled to write this book. It is my desire to share with the world the tools that helped me change my negative mindset.

The first step in changing self-deprecating internal dialogue is identifying it. What has the enemy of the mind been repeatedly saying to you? What has the internal enemy convinced you of that simply is not true?. Answer these questions and move forward.

3

Becoming Your Own Ally

There is a quiet shift that happens when a person realizes they are no longer willing to fight themselves. It does not arrive with fireworks or dramatic declarations. It arrives as clarity. It arrives as exhaustion with old patterns. It arrives as a decision, sometimes unspoken, that the inner war has gone on long enough. This is the moment where self-sabotage begins to lose its grip, not because life suddenly becomes easy, but because the person living it has decided to stop being their own worst enemy.

For many men, women, and children, the most damaging relationship they will ever experience is the one they have with their own thoughts. Long before the world has a chance to reject them, they reject themselves internally. They speak harshly about their abilities, their bodies, their intelligence, and their worth. Over time, those words become beliefs, and those beliefs quietly dictate the choices they make and the risks they avoid. What begins as internal dialogue eventually shapes an entire life.

Self-sabotage thrives in repetition. The repeated thought that says you are not good enough. The repeated joke that downplays your intelligence or talent. The repeated hesitation that stops you from trying again. These patterns often feel normal because they have been practiced for years, sometimes since childhood. Many people do not realize they are sabotaging themselves because it feels familiar, and familiarity can be mistaken for truth.

Children absorb the language spoken around them, but they absorb the language adults speak about themselves even more deeply. When a child hears constant self-criticism, they learn that this is how adults relate to themselves. When they hear hopelessness spoken casually, they learn to expect limitation. This is how cycles continue. This is how generations inherit beliefs that were never theirs to begin with.

Breaking this cycle does not require perfection. It requires awareness and intention. It requires noticing how often you speak negativity over your own life and choosing to interrupt it. Not with forced positivity, but with honesty. Not with denial, but with compassion. The goal is not to pretend struggle does not exist. The goal is to stop reinforcing it with your own words.

Becoming your own ally means learning how to speak to yourself differently. It means acknowledging effort instead of only outcomes. It means recognizing progress even when it feels slow. It means allowing yourself to learn without labeling yourself as incapable. The way you speak to yourself during moments of difficulty matters far more than the difficulty itself.

This work is not limited by age or circumstance. Adults can relearn how to support themselves internally. Parents can model healthier self-talk for their children. Young people can be taught that mistakes are part of growth rather than proof of inadequacy.

Change does not require erasing the past. It requires choosing a different response in the present.

Fear often disguises itself as realism. Doubt often pretends to be wisdom. Self-sabotage often convinces you that staying small is safer than risking disappointment. But safety built on limitation is not safety at all. It is confinement. Growth requires courage, and courage begins with how you speak to yourself when no one else is listening.

You are not required to believe everything you think. Thoughts are not facts. They are habits, and habits can be changed. The moment you realize you have a choice in how you respond to your own thoughts is the moment your power returns. You do not have to silence every negative thought. You only have to stop obeying them.

Being your own ally means choosing self-respect over self-criticism. It means setting boundaries with your inner dialogue just as you would with people who speak harmfully to you. It means recognizing that kindness toward yourself is not weakness. It is strength practiced intentionally.

Life will still bring challenges. Disappointment will still occur. Fear will still visit from time to time. The difference is how you meet those moments. Instead of turning against yourself, you learn how to stand with yourself. Instead of reinforcing defeat, you learn how to steady yourself and move forward anyway.

This book was never about eliminating struggle. It was about eliminating unnecessary suffering. Much of the pain people carry is not caused by circumstances alone, but by the way they interpret and internalize those circumstances. When you change the narrative inside, the external experience begins to shift as well.

As this book comes to a close, understand this truth deeply.

You were never meant to be at war with yourself. You were meant to grow, learn, and evolve with support, including your own. The voice inside you matters. Make sure it is one that guides you forward rather than holds you back.

Choosing not to sabotage yourself is a daily practice. Some days it will feel natural. Other days it will feel uncomfortable. Both are part of the process. Progress is not measured by the absence of struggle, but by the willingness to respond differently when struggle appears.

If you take anything from these pages, let it be this. You are capable of change. You are worthy of compassion, including from yourself. You are allowed to outgrow old beliefs and write new ones. You are powerful enough to become your own ally in a world that often demands too much.

It is the beginning of a different relationship with yourself. One rooted in awareness, honesty, and self-respect. That relationship has the power to change everything.

4

Get to Know Yourself

For us to become aware of our thoughts we first need to slow our lives down a bit. We must take advantage of quiet moments and be still long enough to monitor our thoughts. When you are sitting in traffic, turn the radio off, take a few deep breaths, and begin to notice and acknowledge every thought that comes into your mind. Learning to do this changed my life tremendously. Both good and bad thoughts need recognition. You cannot reverse negative thoughts if you have not taken the time to recognize and acknowledge they exist. Begin by keeping it as simple as taking a mental note of what you are thinking. Start by observing exactly what you are thinking right now. Take ten minutes and detach from everything in the world except your thoughts.

Make a conscious decision to do this every day and, eventually you will see the clear distinction between intentional thoughts versus when our mind runs rampant on its own without any guidance from us. Only then will you notice how many thoughts of fear and impending tragedy run through our minds. These are specifically the thoughts we must learn to dismiss. These are the thoughts that will ultimately cause us harm. It's not horrible to admit you have negative thoughts, on the contrary, it's the first step to a better life. Many will spend years in complete denial. Denying they are even capable of thinking negatively. Negative thoughts exist, just like crime, and while we may not be able to control the crime in the world, we have the power to monitor our thoughts. Stop judging your thoughts as good or bad and re-label them as "thoughts that make you feel good" or "thoughts that make you feel bad." Choosing to label them as good or bad will make you less likely to acknowledge the ones that are not in line with what you desire for your life. Denial and embarrassment will slow down the process. We all think negatively at times. No need to guilt yourself for being a bad thinker. We all have thoughts of fear, failure, anger, sickness, and sadness. You are not alone. You are not a bad person for thinking that way. However, now that you are aware of the damage sustaining a negative thinking pattern can do to your life, it's time to change it. Feel good about being at a place in your life where you are willing to make positive changes towards the betterment of your future. This is the best gift you can give to yourself and others. Learning how to control and change your thoughts will change your life. As human beings we can get so distracted by the ins and outs of our daily routines that most of us rarely even realize that we are thinking all day. Scientists say we have twelve to sixty thousand thoughts per day.

Thoughts come continuously, whether or not we choose to guide them. These thoughts are shaping our daily lives so we must learn to take charge of them. You are what you think all day long. There is no way around it. Our realities are shaped solely by our thoughts. If it's present in our lives, even if we don't remember those specific thoughts, we did indeed think them. We have to learn to create barriers to keep the negative thoughts from penetrating our subconscious mind. We can't avoid thinking, so it's best we take control over this imminent process and manipulate it in our favor. All thoughts travel on energetic frequencies. We are energy as well. Everything in this world is energy, and we have the power to control the energy we put out. Energy exists, no matter what, but we can determine if the energy we emit is positive or negative. If we are entertaining thoughts of disease because someone we know was just diagnosed with an illness and we are now in fear of getting it, then rest assured that our energetic vibration is low at that time.

The good thing is we are in control of the level of energy we put out. We can raise our own energetic vibration at any time. A friend of mine taught me about saging a few years ago. At that point in my life, I was open to new ideas and concepts regarding religion and spirituality. She brought a small piece of sage to my salon and showed me how to use it. I am a person that knows the importance of "belief" in something, so as she was showing me how to rid my body and private spaces of negative energy that can lurk in corners and dark spaces, I set a conscious intention to not reject what she was saying simply because it was foreign to me. Even though it was different and conflicted with my childhood Christian beliefs, I tried to listen and learn with an open mind. I decided that day that the practice of saging was no different than the Christian ritual of taking communion. The drinking of the grape juice and eating of the cracker is also a ritual in remembrance of Jesus Christ and his bodily sacrifice. Communion is a ritual that Christians chose to assign symbolism to. Unfortunately, it was my experience growing up in COGIC (Church Of God in Christ) that only our rituals were accepted, and everything else was considered voodoo or witchcraft. I no longer believe that. I can't say I ever personally bought into the voodoo concept; it was simply the belief of many of the elders that came before me. Most were devout Christians and would have never accepted the belief in healing crystals, burning sage and meditation to open our chakras. Chakras are the centers of spiritual power in the human body.

After my friend was gone I decided to practice what she taught me about saging. I also chose to envision the dark energy leaving through a window and the positive energy coming in. I would say "Negative energy out, positive energy in." As I walk around my salon burning the sage and setting my intentions for positivity and prosperity, I would close my eyes and believe it all as fact. What you believe is what truly matters. You can practice certain rituals but inside you have no faith in them, so they won't work. Many people believe the art of rituals and spiritual ceremonies are evil and demonic. My response to people who say that to me is "That's not what it means to me". Do not allow other people to assign an intention to something you choose to do. For example I am a mother of four and I would allow my children to dress up in customs for Halloween and take part in the parade at school. We would even go from house to house trick- or treating in the evening.

Frequently people have reminded me of some ancient original demonic meaning the Halloween holiday. It never bothered me one bit because that is not what me and my children celebrate it for. We have no evil intent behind our choice to celebrate the holiday nor are we bound by anyone else's. There is always someone who chooses to corrupt something. I choose to see the positive in all things. And any holiday that promotes love and brings people and families closer is OK with me. The choice to participate in something evil is just that, a choice. I'm not interested, and it has nothing to do with me.

The practice of saging became a regular practice in my salon, Braids By SaBrina, which has been my sole source of income for twenty-five years. In September 2019, I changed the name of my salon to "A New Vision Dreadlock Studio." One would think changing the name of a popular business that had serviced the Los Angeles community for so long would not be a great idea, but I sat in stillness for a while and the new name suddenly came to me in less than fifteen minutes. I was fifty years old.

I had recently dealt with some unexpected medical issues that caused me to rethink allowing any form of stress in my life. My staff at my salon were a key source of stress, and at this point there wasn't much of a financial benefit to keeping them around. I felt I had given all that I could to them over the years and now I had to make myself and my health a priority. I made an instant decision to terminate them and change the name of the salon to from "Braids By SaBrina" to "A New Vision Dreadlock Studio." It was a new day and time for A New Vision as I embarked upon the second half of my life. I operated that cute little purple studio for 10 years. I had peace and I made twice the money I made when I had the staff that caused me so much stress.

To this day, I have never regretted my decision. The new salon name came to me so peacefully that I knew it was God telling me to move forward. When we spend time with our mind we will discover answers to questions, solutions to problems will be revealed to us. I started sitting quietly in the empty salon; something I was never able to do when I had employees. I would visualize abundant wealth, and thank God for continued success. I spoke aloud words of gratitude for my business and how consistent it had been. Then I would walk from room to room, saging my beautiful purple salon and speaking my affirmations for both my business and myself aloud. I raised my personal prices considerably and within thirty days of rebranding my salon, I was making double what I made before, even without having a staff. It turned out to be one of the best decisions I have ever made.

Wealth and success can become a reality for anyone who sincerely believes it is possible. I believe that is why I have never experienced poverty. I expect wealth, and yes, I advertise and do all the footwork needed to sustain a small business, but that to me is secondary. My belief that the business could not fail was the primary cause of its continued success. Advertising and promoting a business won't work if subconsciously you believe it will fail. We must see the success in our mind first. God gave us this power as a gift to mankind, but most do not use it. You can experience success in all areas of your life if you first believe it to be possible. All things are possible!. This new practice of saging was just another tool I used to set intentions for peace and prosperity in my life.

There is not one specific tool. Any practice you put complete unwavering belief in will be successful. I'm pleased that I opened my mind and allowed myself to at least listen to other concepts and beliefs and make my own choices. Having that open mind allowed me to be more receptive when I traveled to Bali, Indonesia, Cusco, Peru, Cairo, Egypt, Istanbul, Turkey, and Athens, Greece. In these countries, I visited many monasteries and spiritual temples, which helped to strengthen my belief in one Divine Source.

Different people may package God differently. They may refer to God with a different name, but to me, it's all the same. I respect the amount of reverence that other countries give to honor the creator. I have partaken in many rituals and ceremonies that greatly differ from my Christian church practices. What I've learned is to allow others to worship God the way they choose. It's not my business. If there was a particular practice that resonated with me, I adopted it as my own and moved forward. I feel we get so distracted in pointing out the different way in which we all choose to acknowledge God.

Our ego wants us to be correct. It convinces us that our way is the only way. It's a distraction and a judgment that I don't believe in. To each his own. Who are we to say how another person should acknowledge God? The ultimate universal goal is to live a great life. Learning, growing and evolving in all areas and allowing others to do the same. I do, however, believe that once we fully evolve we don't necessarily need to practice daily rituals to remind us to be positive and speak positivity over our lives. By then, the positive thought process will have become second nature. However, until then, the daily practices that help us keep a positive mental attitude are crucial to having a productive life. They help us form positive daily habits. I was proud that I was able to open my mind and embrace practices that were a definite step out of the C.O.G.I.C. box I was raised in. I have gotten to a point where I enjoy them. I believe strongly in them. I believe they are necessary, and I look forward to doing them daily. I still believe very much in Jesus Christ. I believe he was here to teach us of our Amazing internal power.

I believe that power is what he was referring to as "The Kingdom of Heaven" with-in us all. I will always be eternally grateful for my Christian upbringing. Unlike most I see correlations between Christianity and spirituality. I combine what practices and beliefs work best for my life and move forward. I have convinced myself that taking that small time out of my day to speak positivity over my body, my family, my business, and my life in general is truly the reason I no longer suffer from many of the things a lot of people in this world currently suffer with. I want to teach others how I rid my life of sadness, pain, hopelessness and depression. I get so excited about teaching these practices to others because it is my desire for everyone to learn that their happiness is a choice, and choosing to spend just a little time with your mind can ensure you live a better life.

As far as we know, we only get one mind. Spend as much time with it as possible. View your mind as the cockpit of an airplane. With all the controls clearly accessible and you are the pilot.

Most people don't struggle because the cockpit is broken, they struggle because they're letting anything and everything grab the controls. A random thought becomes turbulence. A simple comment from someone becomes an alarm. Memories can cause storms within us. Then before they know it, they're flying on autopilot, reacting instead of choosing. But the truth is, your mind has instruments for a reason. You can check your altitude, how high or low your emotions are running. You can check your fuel, what type of mental and emotional fuel have you been feeding yourself all day: fear, stress, comparison, resentment... or peace, truth, gratitude, and self-love.

When you spend time with your mind, you start recognizing what every signal is trying to tell you. Sometimes anger is a warning light that you've been ignoring your limits. Anxiety can be your system telling you you're overloaded and need to slow down. When you feel sluggish, is your body asking for rest and release?. Feelings of sadness can mean its time to do a internal self check. You don't have to panic just because a light flashes, you simply have to learn what it means, and respond like a controlled and efficient pilot, not like a frightened passenger.

Because passengers don't control the flight, they just endure it. Pilots stay present. Pilots make adjustments. Pilots don't jump out of the plane when the wind gets rough; they grip the controls, steady the aircraft, and fly through it with wisdom and love. That is what emotional maturity looks like: not a life without turbulence, but a life where you know how to keep your hands on the controls when turbulence shows up.

5

Closing Doors

By the second half of my life, I had learned many tools to control my emotions and to keep myself calm, uplifted and positive. I had read hundreds of self-help books and completely transformed my life from a depressed, angry woman who felt let down by the abandonment of my mother into a confident mother, business owner, artist, author, and positive leader in my community.

I was born to two substance abusers. My mother had a vice for drugs, while my father had a vice for alcohol. My mother was cold, loveless, and abusive, but my father was not. He loved both my older sister and me dearly, often telling us he loved us, as he staggered drunkenly into our bedrooms at night to sit on our beds and attempt to give us fatherly knowledge. He always ended with professing his love for us, his two little girls and only children, who were being raised by his beloved mother, Ella Mae Fisher Fair from Dallas, Texas.

He loved us without a doubt, but he loved alcohol more. My father died when I was ten years old of alcohol-related illnesses like cirrhosis of the liver. While he was in my life for a short time, he did an excellent job of expressing his love for his children: Mary Aurelia and SaBrina Romania Fisher. His name was Jessie Paul Fisher, born in Dallas, Texas on February 28, His mother Ella Mae Fisher Fair and stepfather McClendon Fair brought him and his siblings to California for a better life. I know little about his childhood, but as an adult, he struggled with alcoholism.

I believe having substance abusers as parents kept me from ever abusing any substance. I avoided drugs at all costs. In my forties and fifties, I would enjoy a glass of red wine periodically, but I knew hard alcohol was off limits. I had no desire to be disorientated or out of control. At that time I believed I had a genetic predisposition to addiction, so the overuse of substances was not an option for me. Plus, I saw the horrific impact it had on families like mine and many others. Genetic markers may exist in families, but I believe our minds and strong God-given will have more power. Bottom line: humans are more powerful than they give themselves credit for. You do not have to follow in the footsteps of others just because you share the same blood. You can be just as determined as I was not to succumb to negative addictive vices. My main point is I had numerous reason to be mad at the world. With all that I had been through I easily could have used all my past trauma to act a complete fool and expect sympathy from the world. i chose differently and I want you to do the same.

Learning to be positive is a gift we can give ourselves. It is key in learning to master your emotions. It doesn't mean we are grinning from ear to ear daily and hopping around hugging random strangers and trees. It simply means learning to face each situation, assessing it, even if it is negative, and not allowing yourself to react in a way that causes you and others more pain and suffering. Look deeply into each moment and try to find the positive in it.

For example, imagine a young man showing up to work at a job he loves and has given his best to for over eight years. He is clearly next in line for the supervisor position, and today is the day it will be announced. He wears his best suit and tie, ready to accept his new position and get to work. During the meeting, the director calls a name that is not his. The director calls the name of a man who is hardworking and kind but, in the young man's opinion, not as qualified as he believes he is. He tries to keep his composure, but his heart is broken. He feels let down and overlooked.

These are the moments in life where circumstances seem negative. However, the young man's reaction does not have to be. He could scream, cry, and belittle the man that got the position. He could give a piece of his mind to the decision-makers. He could storm out, make a scene, and express his hurt and disappointment to all the employees. But that is not accessing the situation and finding the positive in it. That is not stopping, breathing, or thinking.

We can't always control the people around us, but we do have full control over our reactions to them. We can't control what happens in every situation because we cannot control other human beings. Maybe if the man who was passed over for the positive took a moment to detach from the emotional sting of it all and truly looked at all sides, he might have concluded that he could have done more. Perhaps his ego convinced him that he was putting in more effort and dedication at his job than he truly was. That doesn't have to be the case, but we need to learn to humble ourselves and look at both sides.

It's also possible that he was indeed the most qualified and that the position simply was not given to him. Even in cases like that, we still must maintain control. We can't allow our minds to tell us lies such as, "You aren't good enough." Putting ourselves down is never the answer. We also can't begin to have negative feelings about another person. We are all phenomenal, and each of us has special talents and gifts. Although it is common to attack ourselves when we get rejected and disappointed in life, continuing this mindset is very dangerous. We are all great and need to develop daily practices to invoke that feeling of greatness inside of us in all situations. There is no shortage of blessings. There is an abundance of blessings for us all. We must learn how to vibrate at the same frequency as them.

Anger and rage are a low-frequency emotions. Fear and self-doubt are also low frequencies. We can't allow our minds to wallow there. Even when we are hurt and disappointed, we must learn how to elevate our vibrations so that we can vibrate at the same frequency as the amazing blessings we desire in our life. Vibrating higher simply means, getting up and intentionally making yourself feel better. Use whatever tools work for you: get up and sing, laugh, dance, read, work out, pray, meditate, recite positive affirmations, whatever will lift your spirit. Do one or a combination of them all repeatedly. Eventually, it will become second nature and a regular part of your life, ensuring you maintain control of your emotions and live a better life than you would have otherwise.

As if staying positive itself wasn't already difficult. Imagine doing it when you have just been diagnosed with an illness. Picture yourself as a positive influencer, acclaimed for authoring the highly successful book titled *"Your Mind is Magic"*. However, you receive distressing news from your doctor: you have a tumor connected to your carotid artery. The surgical procedure to remove it presents two possible outcomes - it can either be a complete success, or a devastating failure resulting in permanent facial paralysis or immediate death due to excessive bleeding. How could one believe that staying positive is possible during times like these? Well, I'm here to convince you that it is. It's far from easy but possible. It requires daily commitment but it is indeed possible. Living in fear is not an option for me. I will enjoy life to the fullest no matter what. As I type this exact paragraph, I am on the Carnival Spirit Cruise ship enjoying a family vacation to Cozumel and Belize!

I have always worked out and maintained consistent exercise habits throughout my twenties, thirties, and forties. By the time I turned fifty on August 7, 2019, other than a few extra pounds and slightly higher than normal blood pressure, I felt I was in good shape. I went in for what was a standard tonsillectomy and adenoid removal surgery. There was also a small cyst in my ear that the doctor was going to remove as well. The tonsillectomy and adenoid surgery went perfectly.

However, when I woke up in recovery, Dr. McAlpin was standing at the foot of my bed, ready to inform me that when she entered through my ear to remove what she believed to be a small cyst, it bled profusely as soon as she made contact with it. She said she immediately realized it was not a cyst but a vascular tumor and informed me I would need another surgery. Over the next few months, I saw a neurosurgeon to prepare for the additional surgery, which was more serious than the initial surgery by the ear, nose, and throat specialist. By this time in my life, I was mastering positive thinking so much so that I had written several self-help books: *My Spiritual Smile: Tools for Mental and Emotional Transformation and Your Mind is Magic: A Guide to Maintaining Positive Thinking. Kicking Depression in the Butt: How to Battle the Internal Enemy and Win, How to Get*

Exactly What You Want From God: Mastering the Art of Effective Prayer, Despite the wonderful new positive mindset habits I had formed, I still had to do a lot of work to not succumb to fear after hearing the news. It was not easy, but it allowed me time to practice the positive tools I so very much believe in.

These tools helped me tackle those days when I did an Internet search on my tumor. These Internet searches would always produce pictures of people with the sides of their heads shaved and deep surgical scars from the front to the back of their heads. I even joined a few Facebook groups for people who had this exact type of tumor, which at the time they believed was an Acoustic Neuroma initially but later they settled on a Glomus Tympanicum. That decision to join that group was not a good idea. Being in the group kept me in a state of fear. Even once I had gotten to where I could resolve the feelings of fear, communicating with people who had unsuccessful surgeries and constantly seeing images of the aftermath and complications was not good for me. So, I left those groups alone.

By May 2023, after the COVID-19 pandemic canceled my scheduled surgery, I felt a twinge of pain in the area where the tumor was located. I created an affirmation for when I meditate. Each time I would feel the pain, instead of getting scared and worried, I would tell myself that the air I was breathing in was healing, restoring, and repairing every cell in my body. The air I was breathing out was releasing all toxins, sickness, and disease from my body. I convinced myself that the periodic pain was the tumor shrinking. This presents a challenge because it opposes logic. However, I strongly believe God has given us the power to heal our own bodies.

I was consistent with my "mindset magic" because I knew I had to reverse my way of thinking, but I knew it was possible.

Mindset magic is the phrase I use to refer to the amazing mental power we all possess, a powerful unseen force we can manipulate for the good. Some call that unseen positive force God. Some may refer to it in other ways. Don't get caught up in the words. Just know that everyone has access to that power; they simply have to tap into it. This amazing energy is also in the words we speak.

I had to adjust my affirmation from: "I Am Healing, Restoring, and Repairing" to "I Am Healed, Restored, and Repaired." It's already done! We must believe and thank God not for what we wish and pray will happen, but we must sustain the unshakable belief that it has already happened. It's a mindset twist, but it works. Believe in the unseen, and it will appear.

Just because a doctor has given us a prognosis doesn't mean we have to fall into a mindset of death and despair. Emotionally I wanted to scream and lose it. But That would have frighten my children and served no positive purpose. I am not saying to stifle normal hurt and disappointment. Cry, cry a river but eventually you must return to some semblance of emotional control. I still had to be a mother. I still had to go to work and pay the mortgage. I did just that. I used the tools I mention in this book to keep myself from drowning in fear.

I attended all of my scheduled appointments and followed all the doctors' orders, as I would advise everyone to do. However, in addition to that, I used visualization techniques to imagine the tumor getting smaller and smaller whenever I listened to this particular sound. The sound I chose was 432 Hz frequency. I learned about binaural beats many years prior and would periodically listen to 528 or 432 Hz binaural tones or Tibetan flute. I find it extremely peaceful and calming, making it perfect for meditation. Since it was familiar to me, I set an intention that every time I heard the tone, my tumor would shrink.

This type of visualization takes consistent work and, most importantly, a strong belief system. The logical mind, will attempt to talk us out of things that don't seem logical, but you must learn to bypass that and stay focused on the goal you are trying to achieve. Not every day will be a good day. On those days, it's especially important to implement the tools you're learning in this book. Some days, you may feel discouraged or have a hard time focusing. At times, it may feel silly, and you might think it's not working. Please do not give up. It takes repeatedly doing something for a while before it becomes a habit. Eventually, you will have practiced being positive so much that it will be a part of your authentic character. You are training your mind to look for the positive in all situations. You are trying to balance your emotions and it is not easy. Find tools as I did that help to keep you calm.

January 2025 almost five years later, my tumor was successfully removed at UCLA hospital in California by Dr. Akera Ishiyama with no major complications. God is Great.

There was a time when one of my adult children went missing. They had not made contact for days, and we were all worried. Although this was definitely cause for concern, in a situation like this, you still cannot allow your mind to take you down a dark road. As the days went by, I began to have thoughts of my child being found dead. I even had visions of being at their funeral. This was a very difficult time for me, but I knew the dangers of allowing myself to be so consumed with fear. I could not lose control of my emotions. I would not have been able to function for my other children. I tried to refrain from focusing on things that had not happened. I prayed and used my vibrational tools to keep me calm.

I understand that fear and worry can make you think horrible things, I get it. Negative thoughts will arise during crises like these, but you simply cannot allow them to linger. While my child was still missing, I consciously had to replace those negative images with positive ones. This is hard to do when you are overwhelmed with worry and concern, but I had to cast out the negative and replace it with the positive, or I would not have been able to get up in the morning. Three weeks later, we found my child alive. There were challenges that they still needed to face, but they were alive to face them. Had I given into those images of death, I believe it might have been different.

If that situation wasn't debilitating enough, a few years later, another one of my adult children went missing. Fortunately, by then, I was even more advanced in my positive thinking habits. After a few days of calling around and trying to piece things together, they were found in another state, though not in the best condition. As hard as that was to handle, I had to acknowledge the positive: they could have been dead. The phone call I received could have been to identify the body, but it wasn't, and for that, I was grateful.

Make no mistake, the conscious choice to stay positive in difficult situations doesn't always ease the pain or dismiss the reality of what's happening. In my case, it kept me from having a mental breakdown, which would have rendered me incapable of helping anyone. Pain is real, and certain life experiences can cause us tremendous suffering. However, if we train ourselves to stop for a moment, breathe, think and gain control of our emotions, we can manage it better. Focus on the thoughts you want to think about, not the uncontrollable ones fueled by fear. If you allow yourself that time, you're more likely to come up with the best solution for the problem. Those moments of silence and reflection can also help us accept the things we cannot change.

Although I know many parents have had to endure this disheartening experience, I do not believe God designed it for a parent to bury their child. Fortunately, despite some touch-and-go moments, as of 2024, all four of my beautiful children are alive and well, and I couldn't be more grateful.

We Are in Control

We must learn to control our emotions and reactions. No one can make you scream, holler, or lash out; you have full control over your behavior, even when someone provokes you and crosses a boundary. We live in a world with other human beings, and we cannot force our will onto them. Sometimes others are downright wrong in how they handle us, and we are justified in our hurt and anger. However, challenging or confronting them puts us in a negative headspace.

Sometimes, it is best to let it go, not only externally, but, most importantly, internally. Talking to yourself and having an imaginary conversation where you are telling the person off is just as damaging as actually confronting the person. Remember "What we think about, we bring about." If we hold on to anger, hostility, and resentment, we are the ones who suffer. We suffer mentally, physically and emotionally.

Internal peace and full control over ourselves is the desired result for us all. In some situations, addressing the person who has hurt, abused, or offended us is necessary and beneficial. However, it is vital to do this from a place of peace. Do not confront others while you are still angry or seeking vengeance. Some people have harmed us whom we may never see again, but we must release the pain associated with them and what they did to us. It is easier said than done, but it is crucial if we want to lead a happy, positive life and keep our minds free of negative thoughts.

Negativity will always exist in this world. There is nothing you can do to rid the world of negativity entirely. You cannot even appreciate the positive if you are unaware of the negative. This book helps you identify negative thoughts and replace them with positive ones. Darkness and light will always be factors in the world. Yin and Yang are realities of this world, no matter what. If only good existed, you would have no comparison. You can only identify good because you have seen and felt what bad is. You choose which area you want to operate in. Every day, you make a choice, even if you do not realize it. You are making a choice!

For example, one day, I had a tension headache, which is common. The week prior had been extremely busy, with long hours at my salon, plus a couple of women's seminars I attended. I also took my kids to the Monster Jam at the SoFi Stadium, which kept us up long past my desired bedtime. When I got the tension headache, instead of simply attributing it to the long, hard week before, I started thinking it was because the tumor in my head was growing. This could not have been further from the truth. I figured since I felt the pain on the left side, near my eye and ear where the tumor was, it certainly must be a side effect of the tumor's growth. This is a dangerous way to think, but these are exactly the examples of negative thinking I want you to identify after reading this book. Allowing yourself to think that way can surely cause your emotions to spiral.

I want you to learn how to "Catch and Cast" catch the negative thought as it comes in and cast it away. Replace it with a positive thought. I knew I had to cast those thoughts right out of my head, and I did. I took two Excedrin, went to bed, and felt wonderful the next day. Allowing myself to use the positive tool that I created kept me from loosing control of my emotions and becoming fearful that in some imminent danger from the tumor.

Identifying each time you slip into that dark-thinking place is the first step to winning the battle against negative thinking. When you notice the regularity of these negative thoughts, please do not feel defeated or disappointed in yourself. Instead, applaud the fact that you can now recognize and control when it is happening. If you do not notice the negative thoughts, you cannot change them into positive ones. Consider it growth that you can notice when your thought pattern has taken a turn for the worse. We can all lead predominantly positive lives, which will allow us to enjoy this beautiful life experience to the fullest. It all begins in our minds,master your thoughts, and you will master your life.

Every day may present a circumstance that can upset you, but you can handle anything. If you are still reading this book then you know that you are the one in control of your emotion and reactions. One day, I took my middle daughter to the dentist. While waiting for her in the car, I used that time to get some writing done on this very book. I knew better than to let the radio play while the car was off, so I did not have the radio on. I waited for about an hour and a half, and when she was done, I attempted to start the car, but the ignition would not start.

The car's computer system had been telling me to replace the battery in my car key, for weeks, but I had not made time to do that because the dealership was far from my home, and I do not like driving distances. It was nearing 10:30 a.m., and I had to be at work at my salon by 1:00 p.m. I started to get annoyed. Then I remembered that all Mercedes-Benz cars come with free roadside assistance for life. I called them, and although it took them about an hour, they came out and started the car.

While waiting, I took a few deep breaths and pushed down the anxious feeling of annoyance when they tried to rise up. I crawled into the back seat and began writing this very paragraph. These are the daily life episodes where we must learn to remain positive. I filled my mind with all the positives in this situation. It could have been much closer to the time I needed to be at work, which would have made me late. It could have been nighttime instead of 10:00 a.m., which would have been frightening for my daughter and I to be stranded at night. I might not have been blessed with free roadside assistance and could have been stranded with my daughter without a plan. It could have been a much worse situation.

It may not always seem like it, but there is a positive in every situation. Sometimes small inconveniences, such as my car not starting up, force us to slow down and take care of important things we may be neglecting. I knew for over a month that the battery in my car key remote was very low. The funny thing is, I had no idea the computer in the car and the computer in the key needed to work together for the car to start. Mercedes Roadside Assistance came right out, started my vehicle, and then my daughter and I drove straight to the dealer, got the new car key batteries, and even picked up a couple of cute Mercedes caps while I was there. All things work out for the good.

I have been in many relationships that have led me to develop negative feelings. When you give your heart, mind, body, and soul to another person and they mistreat you, it can indeed put you in a very negative place. Staying in that dark place can cause you to react in ways that are not productive. Sometimes, we cannot believe the audacity of people who do cruel and disloyal things, especially when we feel we have been good to them. I know firsthand how painful these situations can be.

I have lost control many times when I felt betrayed by a lover, spouse, or even a family member. However, a negative, explosive reaction never produces a good result. While there may be momentary satisfaction, in the long run, you end up feeling worse about yourself for how you responded, which only causes you more pain and suffering. Your reaction does not change the other person's behavior, so it is pointless.

We have all been hurt by others but we still have to learn to control our emotions. The emotions will pass, no matter how extreme they may seem in the moment, and eventually, the situation will not seem so dire. The pain will subside, trust me, it will. We must learn to remember that, even amid negativity, positive things still exist. Be patient with yourself, because all wombs will heal.

I was once one of those hurt people who lashed out when I was in pain. However, there is a better way. There is a way to handle pain and disappointment that will not make you feel horrible about yourself and will not cause another person the very pain you do not want to feel. When someone hurts your feelings, insults you or betrays your love and loyalty, stop and take a breath. Acknowledge how it made you feel. Give yourself time to process and allow those feelings to pass. They will, even though it may seem like they will last forever, they will not.

If you must address the situation, do so calmly and with a level head. Handle it in a way that does not inflict pain on another person. Returning to a place of love does not mean you have to continue engaging with the person or that you are still in love with them. It means you love yourself enough to react in a way that fosters love, not hate. You will always feel better in the end when you choose the positive over the negative. Hate, resentment, and anger can lead to sickness and disease in the body. Remember, positivity is not about perfection. It is about learning to stay positive even when life is not perfect, and that effort is worth it.

We can have a better world despite how horrible things may seem. Yes, hate, greed, crime, sickness, and death exist, along with a host of other horrific things. Yes, unnecessary wars are being fought all over the world, claiming the lives of many innocent people. However, even amid global catastrophes, you can still choose to focus on the positive. It does not make you a bad person to enjoy life while others are suffering from poverty and death. Those harsh realities will always exist, but we do not have to stay focused on them. The bad will always be there, but so will the good. Focus all your energy on the things that make you smile. Find positive tools that help keep you uplifted and in control of your emotions.

6

Depression

What does Depression Really Feels Like? I personally know the feeling very well. When you are depressed you feel hopeless and unloved. You feel that God is not listening or helping you. It can feel that no one understands you and you are all alone in the world. I must first tell you that all of those feelings are valid, and although it may not seem like it at the time. Those feelings of doom and despair will pass. Before you read any further I want you to know that there is hope. I have to ensure you that, you will feel better one day. After darkness there will be light. So Please do not give up.

Depression isn't always loud. Sometimes it whispers. Sometimes it doesn't even feel like sadness at first. It feels like heaviness. Like a heavy weight is sitting on your chest. Like your spirit is wearing wet clothes you can't peel off. It feels like waking up already tired, like your body showed up but your joy forgot to come with you. It feels like moving through life underwater, people are talking, time is passing, responsibilities are stacking, and you're trying to act normal while your insides are quietly screaming, *"I can't do this."*

DEPRESSION

In my early twenties, I experienced depression many times. However, I didn't have a name for it. I was a young Black girl from Compton, California, who had two substance abusers as parents. My father's name was Jesse Paul Fisher, and he loved me and my sister the best he could, but he loved alcohol just a little bit more. He died of alcohol-related illnesses when I was ten years old.

My mother, on the other hand, never seemed to love me or any of the six children she gave birth to. My sister Mary and I were the oldest. Fortunately, we were raised by our father's mother, Ella Mae Fisher Fair. She loved us dearly and treated us well.. However, knowing that my biological mother never wanted me caused me to have extreme self-worth issues that led to severe depression. Back then, I wasn't able to identify it as depression. I truly did not know what was wrong with me. I just knew I was smiling on the outside, but on the inside, I felt worthless and unwanted.

That's one of the cruelest parts about depression: it's not always obvious to anyone else. You can still laugh. You can still get dressed. You can still post a picture. You can still take care of everybody. You can still "handle business." But inside, you feel hollow, like you're existing instead of living. Like something precious has been stolen from you and you don't even know when it happened or how to get it back. You may not even have the strength to explain it. Because depression doesn't come with neat sentences. It comes with fog and days of disorientation.

Depression can feel like guilt with no clear cause. Like shame that makes you second-guess your worth. It feels as if you're failing at life because you're not as "strong" as everyone thinks you should be. It can make the smallest tasks feel like climbing a mountain. Brushing your teeth or washing your face are no longer priorities. Returning a text is too much to ask and folding laundry is just out of the question. You can't seem to get in the shower or eat anything.. You have got brain fog and can't make a solid decision. And then you feel even worse because you're thinking, *"Why can't I just do it?"* Depression turns ordinary life into an exhausting dreaded performance.

I remember when I lived in Los Angeles California on 109th and Normandie. Although I was super young I had already been married and was separated by then from my first husband. He was a great provider but not as great at being a faithful husband. He also didn't mind throwing a punch at me from time to time. Nevertheless, I got married anyway at age 19, I was way too young to know how to navigate feelings or stand up for myself. I was still trying to work through my feelings of abandonment from my mother.

But let me tell you something that can help shift your entire healing process: depression is not your friend. It is not your identity. It's an enemy. It's a thief. It's a liar, and the first step to kicking anything in the butt is recognizing it for what it is, not what it claims you are. I felt If my own mother did not want me then no one would. That was a lie. When you are young and just trying to figure life out you believe the lies of the enemy. The enemy is that little voice in your head that makes you feel less than.

Depression is sneaky. It doesn't walk in and announce itself like, "Hello, I'm depression." and I will be here for two weeks. It comes disguised as "I'm just overwhelmed." Or "I'm just tired." Or "I'm just going through a lot." And yes, life can truly be heavy and overwhelming at times. However that is normal and something most human beings go through. They figure it out and find a solution to the problem and move forward. But when you are depressed you can not envision the solutions. You can not see the light.

Statistically, depression is far more common than most people realize. The World Health Organization estimates that **about 280 million people worldwide** live with depression, which is roughly **5% of adults**. World Health Organization+1 That means in almost every family, every neighborhood, every workplace, and every church, there are people smiling through something they can barely carry. And because depression is so often invisible, many suffer quietly for years, thinking they are the only one, thinking something is "wrong" with them, when really they are dealing with a real and widespread condition that deserves real support and real compassion.

And when depression is left untreated or ignored long enough, it can become deadly. The World Health Organization reports that **more than 720,000 people die by suicide every year worldwide**. World Health Organization In the United States alone, the CDC reports **over 49,000 deaths by suicide in 2023**, which is about **one death every 11 minutes**. That number is not just a statistic, it is someone's child, someone's parent, someone's friend, someone who laughed at the cookout, someone who showed up to work, someone who told everybody, "I'm fine," while privately fighting a war in their mind.

Depression can lead to death because it lies in a way that feels final. It slowly drains hope, then convinces you that hope is not coming back. It distorts your thinking until you start believing your pain is permanent and your life is the problem. It can isolate you from people who love you, silence you when you need to speak, and convince you that you are a burden when you are actually a blessing. That is how the danger grows, not always in one dramatic moment, but through a long season of feeling trapped, unseen, exhausted, and ashamed. Many people will never see the light, unfortunately, and that is heartbreaking. But that is also why I wrote this book, because I want you to know there is another ending available for your story, and you don't have to face this darkness alone.

If you or someone you love is ever in that dead-end place where suicide feels like an option, please reach for help immediately. In the United States, you can call or text **988** for the Suicide and Crisis Lifeline. If you are outside the U.S., your local emergency number or local crisis line can help you right away. You deserve support, you deserve safety, and you deserve the chance to live long enough to see that the lie was not the truth.

Spiritually, depression can feel like you're disconnected from everything good. Like your prayers bounce off the ceiling. It convinces you that you are not important enough for God to listen to you. It causes you to believe that God is far away, and you're the only one left in the room. It can feel like silence when you need comfort the most. And that silence can mess with your mind because it makes you assume the worst: *"Maybe God forgot about me."* Or *"Maybe I'm being punished."* Or *"Maybe I'm not strong enough to be helped."* You will throw everything you did wrong in your own face and make that the reason God doesn't care. None of that Is true, but I understand getting you to the point where you accept and believe that you are a wonderful eternally loved creation of God that he has not abandoned will take some time. So hang in there with me because I have definitely been thee.

But I want to say this gently and clearly: your feelings are real, but they are not always telling the truth. There is a little voice in our head that speaks to us all day long, and when we are depressed, so much of what that voice says is distorted. It tells you you're not enough. It tells you you're alone. It tells you nothing will change. It tells you there's no point in trying. And the scary part is that it can sound like *you*, so you start believing it's truth when it's really just pain talking.

Stay hopeful, because that same inner voice can later feed you the complete opposite narrative. The mind that tells you "you'll never make it" can learn to say "I'm getting stronger." The voice that says "nobody cares" can learn to say "I am loved and supported." The voice that says "this will last forever" can learn to say "this is a season, and seasons change." Some people call that negative voice the devil when it's speaking darkness and defeat, and I understand why its hard to believe, because it tries to pull you away from hope, faith, and your future. But the most important thing I can tell you is this: you are not powerless against it. You are much stronger than you think. I am a living, breathing witness that it can all be turned around for the better.

Through daily positive tools, you can learn to switch that negative inner chatter to something that heals you instead of harms you. You can train your mind the same way you trained it to worry, to overthink, to be fearful, to doubt, and to expect disappointments in your life. You can interrupt the lies and replace them with truth. You can practice new thoughts until they become your new normal. And little by little, that voice that once tried to bury you can become a voice that builds you. Because your mind may be loud right now, but with consistency, support, and spiritual strength, you can teach it a new language, one that leads you back to peace.

There are seasons when your emotions will be louder than your faith. That doesn't mean you don't have faith. It means you're human. It means you've been carrying too much for too long. It means your soul is asking for love and care. Even the strongest people can break. Even the most faithful people can feel lost. Even the most "positive" people can have moments where the light goes dim. Depression doesn't mean you're weak, it means you're wounded, and wounds need attention, not judgment.

Recognizing the enemy also means telling the truth about what you've been through. Depression doesn't always come out of nowhere. Sometimes it's built from years of unspoken pain. Sometimes it's grief that never got processed. Sometimes it's childhood trauma you normalized because you had to survive it. Sometimes it's disappointment after disappointment until your hope gets tired. Sometimes it's betrayal. Sometimes it's rejection. Sometimes it's abuse. Sometimes it's simply the pressure of trying to be everything for everybody while nobody is checking on you. I tell my life coaching clients regularly "You Matter First." You must attend to your own mental, emotional, physical and spiritual need first. If you are weak in all of those areas, you will be no good for anyone else.

Yes, sometimes depression can come from chemical imbalance, hormone shifts, health issues, and stress overload. It's not always one reason. Depression can be layered. That's why you can't heal it by pretending it's not there. You can't out-smile it. You can't out-work it. You can't out-achieve it. At some point, you have to stop running from it and turn around and face it head on. Because what you don't confront will keep controlling you.

I used to go months and months happy as a lark. Then some life experience would happen and Bam! I'm depressed again. Life is going to keep presenting challenging experiences. We must learn to control how we react to them.

Here's what I want you to understand: you are not "crazy"

because you feel this way. You are not broken beyond repair. You are not too far gone. Depression is real, but so is recovery. And even if you can't feel it yet, there is still a part of you that wants to live and be happy. The fact that you opened this book proves that. The fact that you are still here means something. The fact that you are still searching means there is still light in you, even if it's small right now.

Sometimes the first victory is not a big celebration. Sometimes the first victory is simply saying, *"This is depression. This is not me."* Sometimes the first victory is admitting, *"I need help."* It's accepting that what has happened to you is not you. Sometimes the first victory is letting yourself cry without apologizing. Sometimes the first victory is telling the truth after years of holding it in. Sometimes the first victory is recognizing that you have been fighting a battle silently, and it's time to stop suffering in secret. We were not put on earth to suffer. The only person that can control how much you suffer is you.

Let's talk about what depression steals, because you need to know what you're fighting for. Depression steals your appetite for life. It steals your excitement. It steals your motivation. It steals your creativity. It steals your desire to connect. It steals your confidence. It steals your ability to imagine a better future. It can even steal your faith, not by removing God, but by blurring your vision so you can't *see* God through the fog. I absolutely blamed God for it all. Everything that happened in my life destroyed my faith in God. I'm so grateful I lived long enough to learn that God had already given me the tools I needed to get up everyday and feel magnificent about myself and my future.

God is not intimidated by your darkness. You don't have to get "better" before you come to Him. You can call on the Divine

Source from wherever you are. You don't have to clean yourself up to be worthy of comfort. Some of the strongest prayers you will ever pray won't be fancy. They'll be simple. They'll be raw. They'll sound like, *"God, I need You."* They'll sound like, *"Help me make it through today."* They'll sound like, *"Please hold me because I can't hold myself."* God is a unseen Divine spiritual force that created us all, who is always working in your favor. God is not a old wise man in the heaven waiting to judge you. He created you with the power to design a beautiful life for yourself. I want you to think of God as a powerful, positive energy that loves you, and think of the Devil as a powerful unseen energy that hates you. The key is understanding that you have the ultimate control over which one of these energies you give in to.

Recognizing the enemy also means recognizing the patterns. Depression has habits. It isolates you. It convinces you to cancel plans and makes you avoid friends and family. You stop picking up phone calls. It makes you feel like a burden. It makes you feel like nobody understands. It makes you replay old mistakes like a movie that never ends. It makes you romanticize disappearing, not necessarily physically, but emotionally. You stop showing up as yourself. You become a shadow of who you were. And the longer it goes unrecognized, the more "normal" it starts to feel. You start to accept it as your baseline.

But we are not accepting depression as your baseline. We are not making peace with something that is trying to destroy your livelihood and your peace of mind. We are not calling this "Just life" when it's actually a battle for your mind, your heart, and your future.

Depression is what Joyce Meyers called the "Battlefield of the Mind" and Mind is all. I have a little motivational slogan I created about the mind.

MIND: M = Manipulating Ideas **I**=In a **N**=New **D**=Direction

This chapter is your line in the sand, it will teach you to manipulate your inner and outer speech in a direction that serves you best. You will learn tools that assist in turning that darkness into beautiful light. I am speaking from experience. I have survived many different episodes of extreme depression.

This book will help you say: *"I see you, depression. I know what you are. You've been hiding in my tiredness, my numbness, my silence, my irritability, my procrastination, my over-eating, my under-eating, my sleepless nights, my panic, my self deprecating language, my shame, my lack of motivation, my social withdrawal, my constant "I'm fine." But I recognize you now and I challenge you to a fight.*

Once you recognize the enemy, that dark invasive energy, you can stop blaming yourself for being under attack. You can find tools and daily practices that help you fight for your life. You can stop calling yourself lazy when you're actually drained. You can stop calling yourself weak when you've actually been fighting. You can stop calling yourself "too much" when you've actually been carrying too much. You can begin to separate who you are from what you're experiencing and that separation is powerful.

You are not depression. You are not your worst day or your darkest thought. We all have dark thoughts at times. You are not your emptiest moment. What has happened to you is not you. You are not what you may have done to yourself. You are not what you lost. You are not what you fear. You are a phenomenal creation of God with limitless potential.

You are still you, under those covers, under the heaviness in that dark room you don't want to come out of. And I believe with everything in me that the real you is still in there, waiting to breathe again. Waiting to remember how great you are. So it's time to get up and start "Kicking Depression in the Butt." Does not matter if you are a man, woman or child. Get up Now! So as we begin this journey.

I want you to promise yourself something: you will not minimize or attempt to numb your pain, you will allow yourself to feel with the knowing that It will pass and you have control over when it does. You will also not surrender your future. You will stop pretending. You will stop suffering alone. You will start telling the truth about your feeling so that you can begin to heal them. You will start learning and implementing tools that make you feel better. You will start rebuilding your mind. You will start reclaiming your spirit. You will start creating a life that supports your healing, not just a life that looks good to other people.

Because you deserve to feel light again. You deserve to feel hopeful again.

You deserve to enjoy your life again because Life is Beautiful. Depression doesn't get to have the final word. **Not** this time. **Not** with you. **Not** while you're reading this. **Not** while your spirit is still fighting to come back to the surface.

This is the beginning of your transformation and I'm beyond excited for you. Please remember that **You are Great and this is your Life to Create, So Lets Go!**

7

How to Pray

No doubt that prayer works. It does. Prayer is one of the most powerful spiritual technologies ever given to humanity. But to what degree prayer works in your life, that is a different story. Prayer is not a matter of whether God hears you. God always hears you. The real question is whether you are praying in alignment with how spiritual law actually functions.

James 2:26 (KJV)

"For as the body without the spirit is dead, so faith without works is dead also."

Many people fall back and expect God to do it all, even though God has already given them the power to co-create. When you pray and then sit idle, waiting for heaven to drop your desire into your lap without your participation, you may find yourself disappointed. Not because God is withholding, but because you have not stepped into the authority God has already placed within you. You may see less of what you've been praying for actually show up in your life, not because prayer failed, but because you did not pray from your rightful position, as a partner with the Divine.

As I always reiterate: "The Kingdom of Heaven is inside of you." That means God is inside of you. The Divine is not an elderly man in the sky, watching your life from a distance. The amazing, unseen, omnipotent spiritual force that created all things is not visible to the naked eye, but its presence is undeniable. It lives within your body, your breath, your intuition, your imagination, your faith, and your consciousness.

This realization alone can change the entire way you pray.

Most people were taught to pray upward, toward a God "out there or up there." They beg, plead, and hope they sound convincing enough. But effective prayer does not beg. Effective prayer does not bargain. Effective prayer does not wonder.

Effective prayer aligns.
Effective prayer assumes.
Effective prayer believes before seeing.
Effective prayer speaks with authority, not fear.

You do not pray to a God outside of you, you pray **with** the God who lives within you. When you understand that prayer is a partnership, a spiritual collaboration between you and the Divine energy that formed you, something inside shifts. You stop thinking of prayer as a desperate request and begin seeing it as a sacred command, spoken from the divinity within you to the universe around you.

Prayer begins to work consistently in your life when you stop waiting for miracles and start participating in them.

Prayer Is Not Passive - It Is Creative

Most people misunderstand prayer because they think prayer is merely words. But prayer is not just sound. Prayer is intention. Prayer is vibration. Prayer is alignment. Prayer is energy. Prayer is emotional agreement with what you are asking for. You cannot pray for peace while vibrating in anxiety. You cannot pray for abundance while believing you are unworthy. You cannot pray for love while repeating the story of how you never get chosen.

Your words are the surface of your prayer.
Your emotions are the engine of your prayer.
Your belief is the activator of your prayer.

When these three align, word, feeling, and belief, your prayer becomes magnetic. It becomes a spiritual command that the universe responds to.

Prayer works not because God suddenly decides to bless you, but because you began to align yourself with what God already declared possible.

Prayer Without Belief Is Just Noise

Think about it:

How many times have you prayed but secretly doubted?

How many times have you asked God for something but expected rejection?

How many times have you said the right words while feeling the wrong feelings—contradicting with your thoughts what you asked God for?

This is not judgment. This is awareness. I want you to begin to recognize the behavior. You cannot change any habit that is not serving you until you acknowledge it. Prayer becomes ineffective when you speak one thing but believe another.

You cannot say:
"God, please heal me,"
while thinking,

"But I will probably suffer forever."

You cannot say:
"God, bless my finances,"
while believing,
"There's never enough for someone like me."

The universe does not respond to your words alone; it responds to your energetic signature. It responds to your vibrational frequency. Old-school Christians may resist that language, lol, but we are all energy. We vibrate at different frequencies depending on what we are experiencing.

When you are angry, you are vibrating low.

When you are happy and motivated at church on Sunday, stop and feel that energy. It's high. You are vibrating high because church is a tool that makes you feel good.

There is truth everywhere; we must learn to accept the tools others choose, even if they differ from our own. I always say: **"If it's good, it's God."**

If it uplifts you, it's God.

If it warms your heart, it's God.

If it generates love, it's God.

If it leads to harm, cruelty, or destruction, it is not God.

Use that as a barometer to gauge whether you are operating at a lower vibration. And all you have to do is stop, recognize, and make the conscious choice to raise that vibration.

Whether you're singing in church or playing a sound bowl on a mountain, if it brings you joy and peace, **IT IS ALL GOD.**

That is why Jesus said, **"As you believe, so shall it be done unto you."**

He did not say, *"As you wish,"* or *"As you hope."*

He said, **"As you believe."**

Because belief is not just a surface thought – it is a *deep inner agreement*.

And until that agreement reaches the **subconscious mind**, it cannot fully manifest.

Your subconscious is the part of you that stores identity, patterns, emotions, memories, and automatic responses. It is the silent operating system beneath your awareness that accepts whatever you repeatedly think, feel, or say as truth, even when it's not. It is powerful, creative, and obedient. It does not judge your beliefs; it simply carries them out.

So when Jesus says, *"As you believe,"* He is pointing to the level of belief that sinks beyond the conscious mind and settles into the subconscious.

Because once your subconscious accepts something as true, your behavior, your energy, your expectations, and your magnetism all shift to support it.

Conscious thought asks.

Subconscious belief creates.

And when the two finally agree, manifestation becomes inevitable.

Prayer Works When You Work With It

You cannot pray for strength and refuse to release what weakens you.

You cannot pray for direction and then ignore your intuition.

You cannot pray for abundance and keep speaking lack.

You cannot pray for love and continue settling for disrespect.

You cannot pray for a new life while clinging to old habits.

Prayer requires participation.
God will open doors, but you must walk through them.
God will give you ideas, but you must act on them.
God will give you vision, but you must believe it is yours.
God will give you strength, but you must stop choosing weakness.

Prayer is not magic – it is partnership.
Prayer is not wishing– it is aligning.
Prayer is not avoidance – it is activation.

Why Some Prayers Seem Unanswered

When prayer doesn't seem to work, it is **not** because God ignored you.

It is because one of the essential elements of effective prayer was missing:

- **Clarity** - you weren't sure what you truly wanted.
- **Belief** - you prayed with doubt instead of expectation.
- **Emotion** - your feeling contradicted your request.
- **Action** - you prayed for change but stayed in old patterns.
- **Alignment** - your words and energy did not match.

God does not punish you; God teaches you alignment. Unanswered prayer is not denial, it is redirection toward spiritual maturity. It is an invitation to elevate your understanding of how manifestation and divine law work.

Once you learn these laws, prayer becomes consistent, predictable, and powerful.

Prayer Is a Spiritual Technology

When you pray effectively, you are not merely asking, you are creating. Prayer is the original form of manifestation. It is the bridge between divine intention and physical reality. It is how you speak heaven into the material world.

Every thought is a whisper. Every word is a seed. Every feeling is a frequency. Every belief is a foundation. Every prayer is a blueprint.

You don't wait for prayer to work. You work the prayer. You shape your life with intention. You shift your energy with emotion. You speak your desires with authority. And you walk like someone who knows God is with them, not occasionally, but continually. God never leaves your side.

The God Within You Is the Source of Your Power

When scripture says you were created in God's image, it does not mean God looks like you. It means you carry God's creative power within you. You have the ability to speak life, call things forth, visualize outcomes, shift energy, and manifest realities.

God did not give you prayer so you could beg.
   God gave you prayer so you could build.
   God gave you imagination so you could see what is not yet

visible.

God gave you emotion so you could energize what you desire.

God gave you intuition so you could navigate divine pathways.

God gave you words so you could activate spiritual law.

Prayer works because God works through you.

You are not powerless.

You are not waiting on God.

You are awakening to the God within you—and that is not arrogance,

it's Truth.

Mastering the Art of Effective Prayer

To get exactly what you want from God, you must master three things:

1. Speak with Authority

Do not pray as a victim. Pray as a creator.

Your words should reflect faith, not fear.

2. Feel the Prayer as Already Answered

Emotion is your spiritual currency.

Feel it now, and physical reality eventually aligns.

3. Believe Without Contradiction

A double-minded prayer creates double results.
A focused belief creates miracles.
When word, feeling, and belief unite, your prayer becomes a magnet for the very thing you seek.

Effective Prayer Works - Always

Even when you can't feel it.
Even when you can't see it.
Even when nothing in your life reflects what you asked for.
Prayer is a spiritual seed.
Some seeds sprout quickly.
Some grow roots before they grow leaves.
Some take time because the blessing is being built.

Prayer always changes things, and when you learn to pray from the God within you...when you align your intention, your emotion, and your belief...when you speak with authority and walk in expectation...You won't just pray for miracles, You'll live in them.

Because prayer was never meant to be the language of fear, it was meant to be the language of creation.You are not begging the universe to notice you. You are commanding the life that already belongs to you.

Walk in the authority God placed within you. Pray as one who knows. Believe as one who remembers. Expect as one who is aligned. Because the moment you agree with God, the universe must agree with you.

8

You are Worthy

One of the most significant things I had to change before I could live a happy life was believing that I deserved to live one. We may verbally say we want love, happiness and prosperity in our lives but internally many of us don't actually believe we deserve it.

So many things have been implanted into our subconscious minds that we aren't always aware that our mind is working against us. We may sincerely want a loving relationship with a wonderful mate and actually verbally speak of our desire for one, yet internally deep within us is the hidden fear that it will never happen. It may be our life's dream to own a mansion on a hill and we may even speak that aloud regularly to our friends and family, but inside there is unidentified doubt that we will never make enough money to acquire it. Because of that secret doubt, the things we desire may never show up In our lives.

I was always vocal about the things I desired in my life, yet due to the fact that I was an abandoned child, I never felt worthy enough to have them. As mentioned in chapter two, I was abandoned by my drug-addict mother as a three-month-old baby, and because of this fact I never believed I deserved happiness.

When the person who gives birth to you and brings you into this world doesn't see value in you, it's easy to believe you are not worthy of love. I am now certain that is not true but it took years for me to reverse that belief.

Even though I had done really well in business, I still didn't feel valuable. Success alone does not create or sustain happiness. In 1996, on the corner of 65th and Normandie in Los Angeles, CA, I opened Braids by SaBrina. Before this, I had been braiding hair in my home for a living shortly after high school. I used to advertise with bright, fluorescent Braids by SaBrina signs all over the city of Los Angeles. After my high school graduation in 1987, I went to live with my Aunt SaBra. That time is still a blur because graduation was less than a month after the murder of my grandmother. The details of those immediate years after losing "Mama" aren't completely clear to me, but I do remember having lost all faith in God and humanity. I was angry with God for allowing the horrible incident to happen.

I didn't trust anyone and had no idea how I was supposed to proceed with life, nor did I have any desire to. I never attempted to take my own life, but I thought about it constantly. I was extremely unhappy and unsure of what I believed in. Was God real? If so, how could he allow my grandmother to be taken from me that way? With a gun pointed to her head, her last emotion felt most certainly had to be fear. How could such an amazing person die like that and why was I left here to remember it? Having witnessed it gave me no choice but to replay the murder scene repeatedly in my head daily, which caused me unbearable suffering. Part of me felt like I deserved to suffer. Could I have done something to help her that day? Had I not been immobilized with fear could I have attacked my grandfather? Should I have? These were the thoughts that have plagued my mind for years. These were the thoughts that made me want to end my life. The only reason I didn't was because my grandmother had instilled in me the Christian belief that suicide was the "unforgivable sin." I wanted to go to heaven, so no matter how much pain I was in I never actually attempted to kill myself. I simply wished on may occasions that someone else would kill me.

After years of counseling and extensive emotional and mental work I now know that no matter what my mother did and no matter how horrendous the tragedy I witnessed was, I deserve love and there is indeed hope for happiness. I would regularly seek help by visiting a church counselor or psychiatrist and it took what seemed like a lifetime for me to eventually realize that I was indeed worthy of all of the magnificent things this life has to offer.

Not one of these avenues of help was successful until I eventually learned I was continuing the cycle of trauma. I had to accept that my abandonment by my mother and the murder of my grandmother was not my fault. No form of personal development helped me emotionally until I first accepted that I am not responsible for the things that happened to me, and as bad as they were I cannot change the past event.

I once attended a five-day self-help seminar at a hotel with 18 other people of varying ethnicities. I learned from one of the facilitators named, Sam that you "*cannot change the event, but you can change your perception of it.*" This was my first "*Ah-ha Moment,*" as Oprah calls it. I could change how I perceived the horrible events of my past. I had no idea that his was even possible.

I remember signing up for the seminar around 2009. It was quite expensive, approximately $2000, yet I remember thinking that I had nothing to lose, so why not? Therapy and church counseling weren't working. I was at a point where "Just pray about it" wasn't sufficient. I will admit that the first two days of the seminar my attitude was horrible. I did not believe anyone could help me, and I wasn't looking forward to the looks of shock and pity that I had experienced in the past after sharing my story. After a verbal altercation with another one of the seminar attendees, and another complete day of total resistance, I had a breakthrough. We were given an exercise where we were required to dress to reflect three facets of our personalities. A staff of twenty people had observed us over for a two-day period, and from watching us they were able to identify specific character traits. We were all called up individually and given three characters and told to return tomorrow with costumes, ready to act the part. My three characters were Heidi Fleiss, Etta James and Cupid. I completely understood how and why they picked Heidi Fleiss. In my previous two days there I had been nothing but distant, and when I did speak it was with a very stern, dominant demeanor. I was a stern business owner, and at that time I had employed over 1000 women since I opened my place of business in 1996. I prided myself on being a strong, dominant dictator. At my salon, it was my way or the highway. I understood and embraced the first character, but for the life of me I did not see how they could have possibly seen Etta James or Cupid inside of me. Yet somehow they did, which made me quite emotional.

  I acted out the part of each character. I wore a long, beautiful dress and put my hair up and did a lip sync routine to "Trust In Me," by Etta James. I put on a black business blazer and slacks and readily took on the role of Heidi Fleiss. Lastly, I wore a red outfit and with a bow and arrow and mimicked the Cupid character, still shocked I was even given this part. How could they possibly have seen love in me? Apparently they did. I didn't even see love in me. Once I lowered my defenses and embraced the exercise, I was forever changed by my experience there. I believe it was the catalyst of change for me. It launched my personal development journey.

From this experience with what was then called CEC Seminars, I learned why and how my Heidi character was created. What was most significant to me was when Sam told me, "*Most people throughout your life have told you that you needed to get rid of that strong Heidi Fleiss personality, but I understand why you made her. Many times throughout your life you needed her for survival, but wear her like a coat. When you need that coat put her on but when you don't it's OK to hang her on the coat rack.*"

This changed my life. Sam made me feel that he understood me and all my antics. He didn't dismiss me and write my behavior off as that of the stereotypical "*Angry Black Woman.*" He taught me that there are reasons why we create specific parts of our personality, but we don't need each one daily. He also helped me understand that I can not change the fact that my mother abandoned me but I can change how I perceive the event. Until recently, I had perceived it as a direct attack on my worth when it had absolutely nothing to do with me. I have always been worthy of life. Even as I lie there in that suitcase as a helpless three-month-old baby gasping for air. I was worthy then, and I have a purpose for my life. I believe my life was spared so I could fulfill that purpose.

Everyone deserves love and happiness despite what they have been through. It took me forty years to believe that my life had value. I wrote this book so others dealing with similar circumstance don't have to wait as long.

***"Happiness is the art of never holding in your mind the memory of any unpleasant thing that has passed"* -Buddha.**

In the CEC Seminars, I learned the importance of affirmations. They are one of the tools are used to encourage and convince myself that I was deserving of everything I desired was daily affirmations.

I forced myself on many occasions to literally stand in front of a mirror and say these affirmations repeatedly:

I am perfect.
I am loved.
I am Worthy.
I am healthy and wealthy in all areas of my life.

I continued to speak these affirmations out loud and silently until I began to believe them. Initially, your affirmations may feel like lies, but keep saying them over and over until they become fact. I pushed the idea of into my mind until they stuck. I fell asleep listening to them. I woke up to them as a morning alarm.

Words are powerful and we have the power to speak things into existence. I eventually stopped referring to myself as a abandoned and abused child. I was no longer that.

We have the power to reprogram any subconscious negative beliefs. We can re-train our brain with repetition and emotion. Earl Nightingale says,

"Whatever we plant into our subconscious mind and nurture with

repetition and emotion will become a reality."

9

Demand Happiness

Most people have been conditioned to approach God from a position of smallness. We were trained to beg, plead, wait, wish and hope instead of believe, speak, and expect. Somewhere along the way, many were taught that wanting "too much" was greedy, that expecting abundance was prideful, and that desiring more than mere survival was somehow un-spiritual. That is all non-sense.

Without realizing it, people learned to shrink their prayers to match their fears instead of expanding their faith to match God's promises. We learned how to endure, but not how to demand. Yes, I said demand.

One of the scriptures most often used to support this quiet poverty mindset is, "It is easier for a camel to go through the eye of a needle than for a rich man to enter the kingdom of heaven." - Matthew 19:24. This verse is repeatedly taken out of context and used to convince believers that wealth itself is sinful. As a result, many , many Christians unconsciously develop guilt around prosperity, success, and abundance. They begin to associate holiness with lack and righteousness with struggle. But God never glorified poverty, He glorifies purpose, growth, and wise stewardship. God does not celebrate restriction;

God celebrates expansion that is rooted in love, integrity, and conscious alignment with divine truth. The truth is, the Bible is filled with men and women who were richly blessed and deeply favored by God: Abraham, Joseph, David, Solomon, Esther, Lydia, none of them were called to live small, fearful, or deprived lives. They were entrusted with influence, resources, authority, and responsibility because their hearts were aligned with God's will. Wealth was not their god, but it was a tool God used through them. The problem was never riches, the problem has always been misplaced identity and misplaced devotion.

When you shrink your desires out of fear of being "too much," you do not become more spiritual, you become more limited. Prosperity is available to all who believe it is possible. When you suppress your God-given hunger for expansion, you suppress part of the divine nature placed inside of you. Desire itself is not sin.

Desire is energy. It is creative force. It is the signal that you were designed to grow, to build, to expand, and to steward more. God placed those desires in you on purpose.

This chapter is about reclaiming the sacred right to want more, and to want it without shame. It is about learning how to demand your desires with faith instead of apologizing for them in fear. It is about understanding the difference between greed and God-given ambition, between ego and divine assignment.

You were never created to live timid in your asking. You were created to speak boldly, believe deeply, and expect fully. Demanding your desires is not arrogance. It is your right. It is alignment. When your desires are aligned with God's purpose, your confidence no longer feels sinful. it feels sacred.

So we learned to whisper our dreams instead of speaking them with authority. We learned to ask timidly instead of declaring boldly. Somewhere along the way, faith became passive instead of powerful.

But the truth is this: God already gave you the power to have what you desire. We are not waiting on God. God is waiting on us. The Kingdom of Heaven is within you and always has been. Respecting God does not mean shrinking yourself. Yo do not have to be poor to have Gods favor. Honoring God does not mean living beneath your potential.

In fact, one of the greatest ways to honor divine creation is to fully use what God placed inside of you. Do not believe that you were created to be powerless. You were not created merely to endure life. You were created to demand out of life what you desire. You are here to create, and expand in partnership with the Divine.

For generations, religion trained people to believe that God sat somewhere far away, up in the heavens looking down on us, deciding who was worthy and who was not. That belief kept people in a posture of submission without authority. Yet Scripture itself tells us that we were made in God's image and likeness. That means we were created with creative power, not just obedient silence. You have not because you ask not, and even when most people ask, they often ask like beggars instead of heirs.

Demand Your Desires is a difference between humility and helplessness. Humility says, "I trust God." Helplessness says, "I have no power." God never intended for you to believe that you had no power. To demand your desires does not mean you disrespect God. It means you agree with God about who you are. It means you stop questioning whether you deserve what God already authorized you to have. It means you stop living as if everything is up to chance and start living as if your thoughts, words, and inner images truly matter, because they do.

If it is a new home you desire, God has already said it is yours, but the feelings of disbelief and unworthiness you carry within may be the very barriers keeping it from manifesting just yet. All things are possible, yet for those possibilities to take physical form in your life, doubt must be released.

This is not an easy process, but anything practiced with repetition eventually becomes second nature. Begin to intentionally form positive, habitual thought patterns that work in your favor. We all unconsciously develop negative habits over time, now it is time to consciously reverse that behavior and replace it with faith-filled expectation.

Speak, "I am a new homeowner," not "I will be," but "I AM." The I AM statement is one of the most powerful tools in your spiritual toolbox. Use it with awareness and authority, and watch what you have been asking God for begin to show up in your life.

I AM successful.

I AM a business owner.

I AM a new car owner.

Here is an I AM affirmation I created for my own life and use regularly: " I AM Perfect Health, Abundant Wealth, and covered in God's Divine bubble of protection daily." I need to feel safe while driving and navigating this world with my children so I say this one a lot.

Design one that aligns with your own life and desires and speak it repeatedly. Record it on your phone and listen to it while driving. Play it as you fall asleep. Allow it to quietly seep into your subconscious mind. This is one of the true keys to getting exactly what you want from God.

This is where faith becomes active instead of passive. This is where prayer becomes partnership instead of pleading. The universe responds to clarity, confidence, and consistency. It responds to belief that is rooted and certain, not shaky. It responds to identity that is owned, not apologized for.

Belief speaks. Belief expects. Belief positions itself to receive. Most people are still begging for what they should be commanding. They pray, but they never visualize. They hope, but they never decide. They ask God to intervene, but they never align their own mind with the outcome they say they want. Begging keeps you emotionally waiting. Demanding your desire places you in spiritual alignment. Alignment is where manifestation begins.

To demand your desire, you must first see it clearly in your own mind. Visualization is not fantasy; it is preparation. Imagination is not childish; it is the workshop of creation. Everything ever built in the physical world began as an inner image first. God created through vision and word, and you create the same way.

When you repeatedly visualize what you want, you are not just daydreaming. You are training your subconscious to accept that reality as normal. And what the subconscious accepts as normal, your body and behavior begin to move toward automatically.

When you imagine yourself in great health, you begin making choices that support health. When you visualize unlimited abundance, you begin thinking differently about opportunity and worth. When you picture yourself in peace, conflict loses its grip on you.

Your outer life begins to adjust to match your inner world.

You do not demand from God, you demand through God and the power that he has already granted you. Your words are not just communication. They are instructions to your future.

Every time you speak defeat, your mind takes notes. Every time you speak faith, your subconscious receives authority. Faith does not require proof first. Proof follows faith. To demand your desires also means you stop negotiating with doubt. You stop allowing yesterday to dictate today. You stop letting past disappointment convince you that future joy is unrealistic.

If God brought you through everything you have already survived, why would you believe your future is meant to stay small? You were not preserved for mediocrity. You were preserved for expansion.

We spend so much emotional energy fighting people, situations, and circumstances. We hold grudges. We replay old conversations. We argue silently in our minds with people who may not even be thinking about us anymore. These external battles consume us. But the real enemy has never been outside of us. The real enemy has always been within.

Your true enemy is the voice in your head that tells you you are not enough. The voice that reminds you of your failures. The voice that shrinks your dreams before you even try. Religious people often call this voice the devil. Philosophers call it the ego.

But regardless of what name you give it, one truth remains the same: everything that voice tells you is not the truth. It is fear speaking. It is conditioning speaking. It is memory speaking. It is not God.

You do not defeat the enemy by fighting people. You defeat the enemy by mastering your thoughts. You do not cast out darkness by arguing with it. You replace it with light. The battlefield is in the mind. When the war is won within, external enemies lose their authority over you. When you win the internal battle ofself worth and self sabotage, no out side enemy can even phase you.

Many people blame every setback on the devil while unknowingly entertaining the very thoughts that empower that negative force. That dark energy can not live without you fueling it. The truth is, un-managed thoughts do more damage than any external force ever could. This is why scripture tells us to renew the mind. This is why faith requires discipline, not just emotion.

The first step in declaring war over the internal enemy is awareness. You begin to listen to what you tell yourself in quiet moments. You begin to notice which thoughts drain your energy and which thoughts restore it. And slowly, through intention and practice, you begin to replace the lies with truth.

Replace the negative thoughts with positive ones. Do this repeatedly until it become second nature.This is not just psychological work. This is spiritual warfare. It is the only battle that truly matters. You are defending the territory of your destiny. This is your life and you must take full control of it. So the use of the word demand is not harsh its necessary.

When you stop begging God and start declaring, something shifts in your identity. You no longer see yourself as someone waiting on a miracle. You recognize that you were created as a vessel through which miracles move. You were created in the image of God. Stop seeing yourself as at the mercy of circumstances and begin to see yourself as a participant in the creation of your life.

Desire is not sinful. Desire is not shallow. Desire is the divine signal inside you saying it is time to grow. It is making use of your God-given free will. It is God's way of drawing you into expansion and growth so that your days upon this earth can be abundant in all areas.

To demand your desires is not arrogance. It is agreement with Heaven. So take a moment, close your eye, breath deeply and get clear about what you want for your life See it without guilt. Imagine it without fear.

Speak it without apology. Expect it with faith and knowing. Then live as though it is already rearranging itself toward you and soon you will be able to see, feel and live it.

Because in the realm where God works first, the unseen, it is

already done. The moment you fully believe that, the war is over.

10

The Quiet Ways We Undermine Ourselves

Self-sabotage does not always show up as chaos or obvious destruction. In fact, some of the most damaging forms of self-sabotage are quiet, polite, and socially acceptable. They hide behind responsibility, loyalty, patience, and even kindness. They do not look like failure from the outside. They look like endurance. They look like someone who keeps going even when they are exhausted, someone who shows up even when they are depleted, someone who stays silent even when something inside them is screaming to be heard.

Many people believe self-sabotage is loud, reckless, or dramatic, but more often than not it is subtle. It shows up in the way you delay your own needs, minimize your own discomfort, or rationalize situations that drain you emotionally. It lives in the choices you make when you know better but feel obligated to choose familiarity over growth. It is not always about what you do wrong. Sometimes it is about what you never allow yourself to do at all.

There is a version of self-sabotage that looks like being overly understanding. You make excuses for people who consistently disappoint you. You tell yourself they are doing the best they can while quietly ignoring the fact that you are doing more emotional labor than you can sustain. You convince yourself that asking for more would make you difficult or ungrateful. Over time, this pattern teaches you to betray your own truth in the name of keeping the peace, and the cost of that peace is your emotional well-being.

Another quiet form of self-sabotage is waiting. Waiting for the right moment, the right mood, the right level of confidence, or the right amount of validation before you act. Waiting feels safe because it postpones risk, but it also postpones growth. Life does not reward hesitation the way we wish it would. Clarity often comes after action, not before it. When you consistently wait for certainty, you unknowingly train yourself to remain stagnant while life continues to move forward without you.

Self-sabotage also thrives in overthinking. You replay conversations, analyze decisions, and imagine outcomes that have not happened. You exhaust yourself mentally while telling yourself that you are being responsible or prepared. In reality, overthinking is often fear wearing the mask of intelligence. It keeps you busy without allowing you to move. It creates the illusion of control while quietly eroding your confidence in your own judgment.

Many people sabotage themselves by clinging to identities that no longer fit. You continue to see yourself as the person who struggles, the one who sacrifices, or the one who never quite gets ahead. Even when your life begins to change, that identity lingers, influencing your choices and expectations. Growth requires releasing outdated versions of yourself, and that release can feel unsettling. There is comfort in familiarity, even when familiarity is painful.

Another overlooked form of self-sabotage is neglecting rest. Hustle culture has convinced many people that exhaustion is a badge of honor. You push through fatigue, ignore your body's signals, and tell yourself that slowing down would mean falling behind. In reality, chronic exhaustion clouds judgment, weakens emotional resilience, and increases the likelihood of self-destructive decisions. A tired mind is more likely to settle for less, tolerate dysfunction, and abandon long-term goals for short-term relief.

Self-sabotage often shows up in the stories you tell yourself about what you deserve. If you believe that love must be earned through sacrifice, you will choose relationships that require you to give more than you receive. If you believe success is reserved for other people, you will unconsciously undermine opportunities that could elevate your life. These beliefs do not always feel like beliefs. They feel like facts, especially when they have been reinforced by past experiences.

There is also a form of self-sabotage rooted in loyalty to pain. When you have lived through hardship, struggle can become familiar territory. Healing, joy, and stability may feel foreign or even uncomfortable. You might find yourself unconsciously recreating patterns that mirror past wounds because they feel predictable. This is not because you want to suffer. It is because your nervous system has learned how to function in survival mode and does not yet trust peace.

Emotional self-sabotage frequently appears in the way you speak to yourself. The internal dialogue you carry shapes your perception of reality. When your self-talk is harsh, dismissive, or critical, it becomes difficult to take healthy risks or believe in positive outcomes. You may outwardly encourage others while privately tearing yourself down. Over time, this inner environment becomes toxic, even if your external life appears stable.

Boundaries are another area where self-sabotage quietly takes root. Saying yes when you mean no, tolerating behavior that makes you uncomfortable, or avoiding difficult conversations to keep others comfortable all chip away at self-respect. Each time you override your own needs, you reinforce the belief that your feelings are less important than someone else's convenience. That belief does not stay contained in one area of life. It spreads.

There is also self-sabotage in constantly comparing yourself to others. Comparison distorts reality and robs you of presence. It shifts your focus outward instead of inward, making it difficult to recognize your own progress. Everyone's path unfolds differently, yet comparison convinces you that you are behind or lacking. This mindset fuels insecurity and discourages persistence, even when you are making meaningful strides.

Fear of success can be just as paralyzing as fear of failure. Success brings visibility, responsibility, and change. If you associate success with loss, criticism, or abandonment, you may unconsciously avoid it. You might downplay achievements, decline opportunities, or sabotage momentum just as things begin to improve. This behavior is rarely intentional, but it is powerful.

Self-sabotage is often reinforced by unresolved guilt. Guilt convinces you that wanting more is selfish or undeserved. It whispers that your happiness might come at someone else's expense. When guilt goes unchecked, it influences decisions in subtle ways, leading you to choose paths that feel familiar rather than fulfilling.

One of the most significant steps in breaking self-sabotage

is learning to notice patterns without judgment. Awareness is not about punishment. It is about understanding. When you observe your habits with curiosity instead of shame, you create space for change. Shame keeps you stuck. Compassion creates movement.

Healing from self-sabotage requires honesty. It asks you to acknowledge where you have been standing in your own way, not to criticize yourself, but to reclaim your power. Every pattern you recognize is an opportunity to choose differently. Change does not happen all at once. It happens in moments, decisions, and small shifts in awareness.

There will be discomfort when you stop sabotaging yourself. Growth often feels unfamiliar before it feels empowering. You may second-guess yourself, feel exposed, or experience resistance from others who are accustomed to the old version of you. These reactions are not signs that you are doing something wrong. They are signs that you are changing.

Learning to support yourself requires practice. It involves speaking to yourself with the same patience you offer others, honoring your limits, and trusting your intuition. It means allowing yourself to outgrow roles, relationships, and narratives that no longer serve you. It means choosing alignment over approval.

Self-sabotage thrives in silence, but it weakens in awareness. The more you understand your patterns, the less control they have over you. You do not have to eliminate every limiting belief before moving forward. You simply have to be willing to notice when one shows up and choose a different response.

This chapter is not about perfection. It is about recognition. It is about understanding that the ways you have undermined yourself were learned responses, not character flaws. And anything learned can be unlearned.

As you approach the final chapter of this book, consider this moment a pause. A moment to reflect on what you are ready to release and what you are willing to do differently. You are not here by accident. You are here because some part of you is ready to stop standing in your own way.

The work does not end here, but it does shift. What comes next is not about fixing yourself. It is about trusting yourself enough to move forward without self-betrayal. That is where true change begins.

11

Choosing Yourself: Ending the War Within

There comes a point in every person's life when the greatest threat is no longer what happened to them, but what they continue to say to themselves because of it. For many of us, the harshest voice we will ever hear does not come from the outside world. It comes from inside our own minds. It is the voice that tells us we are not good enough, not smart enough, not capable enough, or not deserving of happiness. Over time, that voice becomes familiar, and familiarity can be mistaken for truth. This is where self-sabotage quietly takes root.

    Men, women, and even children learn early how to speak negatively about themselves, often without realizing they are doing it. They repeat phrases they once heard spoken over them. They internalize labels that were never meant to define them. They casually dismiss their own abilities with jokes, sarcasm, or self-deprecating language, not understanding that words shape identity. What begins as an offhand comment becomes a belief. What becomes a belief eventually becomes behavior. This is how people unknowingly stand in their own way.

Negative self-talk does not protect you. It does not make you humble. It does not prepare you for disappointment. It slowly erodes confidence, limits imagination, and convinces you to settle for less than you are capable of becoming. When you repeatedly tell yourself that you cannot do something, your mind accepts that instruction. When you constantly speak defeat over your own life, your nervous system responds as if that defeat is inevitable. The body listens to the mind, and the mind listens to the words we choose.

This pattern affects every age and every gender. Men are often taught to suppress emotion, leading to internalized frustration and harsh self-judgment. Women are frequently conditioned to doubt themselves, apologize unnecessarily, or shrink to make others comfortable. Children absorb everything, especially the way adults speak about themselves. When they hear constant self-criticism, they learn that it is normal to diminish themselves. What we say about ourselves becomes what the next generation believes about themselves.

Ending this cycle requires intention. It requires awareness. It requires a willingness to challenge thoughts that feel automatic but are not accurate. You must begin listening to how you speak to yourself when no one else is around. Pay attention to the phrases you repeat internally. Notice how often you say things like "I can't," "I'm terrible at this," or "I'll never get it right." These statements may feel harmless, but they quietly reinforce limitation. They teach your mind to expect failure instead of possibility.

Choosing not to be your own worst enemy does not mean pretending life is easy or ignoring your struggles. It means refusing to define yourself by them. It means speaking to yourself with the same patience and encouragement you would offer someone you love. It means understanding that mistakes are part of growth, not evidence of inadequacy. When you replace self-criticism with self-awareness, you create room for change.

This work is especially important when life has been hard. Trauma, loss, and disappointment can distort self-perception. They can convince you that pain is a reflection of your worth rather than a circumstance you endured. But suffering does not diminish your value. It reveals your resilience. The fact that you are still here means something inside you has already chosen survival. The next step is choosing self-respect.

Teaching yourself to speak differently about your life is not about forcing positivity. It is about accuracy. It is about recognizing your ability to learn, adapt, and grow. It is about acknowledging effort instead of only outcomes. When you say, "I'm learning," instead of "I'm failing," your nervous system responds differently. When you say, "I'm capable of figuring this out," instead of "I'm not smart enough," your mind remains open instead of shutting down. These shifts may seem subtle, but they are powerful.

This book was written to remind you that you are not broken, lazy, or incapable. You are human. And being human means having the ability to change how you think, speak, and respond. It means having the capacity to interrupt old patterns and choose new ones. Self-sabotage thrives on repetition and unconscious behavior. Awareness disrupts it. Choice dismantles it.

As this book comes to a close, I want you to understand something deeply. The goal is not perfection. The goal is consciousness. The goal is to catch yourself when you are about to tear yourself down and choose a different response. The goal is to model healthier self-talk for the people watching you, especially children who are learning how to see themselves through your example.

You do not have to be free from doubt to move forward. You only have to stop letting doubt be the loudest voice in the room. You do not have to feel confident every day. You only have to refuse to speak cruelty over your own life. The way you talk to yourself matters. It shapes your reality more than you may realize.

This is where the cycle ends. Not because life suddenly becomes perfect, but because you decide to stop fighting yourself. You decide to become your own ally instead of your own obstacle. You decide that growth is possible, healing is available, and your words will no longer work against you.

If you take nothing else from this book, take this truth with you. You are not your past. Nor are you your mistakes. You are not the limiting beliefs you once accepted as fact. You are capable of learning, changing, and creating a life that reflects who you truly are. The moment you stop sabotaging yourself is the moment your life begins to open.

This is not an ending. It is a beginning shaped by awareness, intention, and self-respect. That choice belongs to you.

About the Author

SaBrina Fisher Reece writes self-help books rooted in emotional healing, personal growth, and spiritual awareness. Her work blends lived experience with motivational insight, often exploring themes of balance, resilience, self-mastery, and the unseen forces that shape our thoughts and behaviors. Drawing from both practical reflection and metaphysical concepts, her writing encourages readers to develop greater self-awareness, reconnect with their inner strength, and create more intentional, aligned lives.

You can connect with me on:
- https://www.instagram.com/sabrinafisherreece
- https://www.facebook.com/BraidQueenSaBrinaReece

Also by SaBrina Reece

For more than twenty-six years, she built one of the most influential braiding salons and schools in Los Angeles, **Braids By SaBrina**, earning statewide recognition as *"The Braid Queen."* Her success was self-made, built through discipline, resilience, and vision, often without consistent support or validation from others.

Shaped by early abandonment, profound loss, and hard-earned self-trust, SaBrina's life journey led her to explore emotional healing, spiritual alignment, and self-mastery. Today, she is an author, speaker, and guide dedicated to helping others develop inner balance, confidence, and emotional strength.

She is the author of numerous self-help and transformational works, including *My Spiritual Smile*, *Your Mind Is Magic*, *Perfectly Positive*, *Spiritual Balance*, *Living Life on a Higher Frequency*, *Become Your Own Cheerleader*, *Kicking Depression in the Butt*, *Self Sabotage*, *How to Get Exactly What You Want From God*, When I Say "I Am"

The Balance & Focus Series is designed to help readers return to themselves in a world that constantly pulls them off center. These books explore two essential elements of a grounded, intentional life: inner balance and conscious focus.Balance examines how alignment between mind, body, and energy creates stability, emotional clarity, and resilience, even during life's most challenging moments. Focus builds on that foundation by exploring the power of attention, intention, and mental discipline, showing how clarity and direction shape the outcomes we experience.Together, these books offer practical insight and spiritual awareness for those seeking to live with greater purpose, presence, and self-mastery. This series is not about perfection, but about learning how to steady yourself, direct your energy wisely, and create a life that feels aligned from the inside out.

Unbroken

Unbroken: Mending the Holes Left by Life is a deeply honest exploration of healing after trauma, loss, abandonment, and emotional pain. This book is for anyone who has survived experiences that left invisible wounds and wondered if wholeness was ever possible again.

Through personal reflection, spiritual insight, and emotional awareness, SaBrina Fisher Reece examines how unresolved pain creates "holes" in the heart and mind, shaping our thoughts, reactions, relationships, and sense of self. Rather than approaching healing through blame or denial, *Unbroken* invites readers to understand their wounds with compassion and learn how to begin mending them from the inside out.

This book explores themes of emotional balance, self-awareness, forgiveness, spiritual grounding, and the power of the mind to either trap us in the past or guide us toward freedom. SaBrina shares her journey of survival, growth, and transformation, illustrating how it is possible to build a meaningful life even while carrying pain, and how healing does not require perfection, only honesty.

Unbroken is not about pretending life did not hurt. It is about learning how to live fully without allowing past trauma to control the present. It is a guide for those ready to stop surviving and start healing, reclaim their inner strength, and reconnect with the love that has always existed beneath the pain.

If you have ever felt fragmented, overwhelmed, or defined by what you endured, this book will remind you of a powerful truth. You are not broken. You are becoming.

SMALL Business Basics

SMALL Business Basics

SaBrina Fisher Reece is a Los Angeles-based entrepreneur, author, and motivational mentor with more than 30 years of hands-on experience in small business ownership. She built her first company, Braids By SaBrina, at the age of 26 and went on to successfully launch and manage multiple thriving businesses, including A New Vision Dreadlock Studio, Inked 4 Life Tattoo Studio, and Just-In Time Barber Shop. Her leadership philosophy blends faith, discipline, and compassion, resulting in decades of sustained success in some of the most competitive industries.

As an author, SaBrina writes with honesty, clarity, and heart-drawing from her lived experiences to empower readers spiritually, mentally, and financially. She is also the author of My Spiritual Smile, How do I Control My Emotions? Your Mind Is Magic, Living Life on a Higher Frequency, Over 50 and Still Fine - Looking to Date Again, Perfectly Positive, and How to Get Exactly What You Want From God.

Through her books, coaching, and entrepreneurial journey, SaBrina continues to inspire others to create the life and business they deserve, proving that with faith, strategy, and consistency, "all things are possible."r, and motivational mentor with more than 30 years of hands-on experience in small business ownership. She built her first company, Braids By SaBrina, at the age of 26 and went on to successfully launch and manage multiple thriving businesses, including A New Vision Dreadlock Studio, Inked 4 Life Tattoo Studio, and Just-In Time Barber Shop. Her leadership philosophy blends faith, discipline, and compassion, resulting in decades of sustained success in some of the most competitive industries.

PROFOUND
Introduction to the Profound Series

This series was not written to convince you of anything.

It was written to remind you of something.

For most of my life, I searched for answers the same way many people do. I looked outward. I prayed, studied, worked, endured, and tried to become better by force. I believed growth meant effort alone and that transformation required suffering. I was taught, as many of us are, what to believe, what to question, and what to avoid.

What I did not realize at the time was that I was not missing faith.

I was missing understanding.

The *Profound Series* was born from a deeply personal journey of self-discovery, healing, and expansion. It is the result of decades of reading ancient texts, studying metaphysical teachings, reflecting on spiritual principles, and most importantly, applying this wisdom in real life. This series is not meant to replace religion, tradition, or belief systems. It is meant to widen the lens.

Religion offers structure, community, and devotion. Ancient wisdom offers context, depth, and responsibility. Together, they reveal something powerful: that you are not separate from the divine, and you were never meant to live disconnected from your inner power.

This series exists because I discovered that much of what we are seeking has already been known for centuries. Long before modern psychology, neuroscience, or self-help, ancient philosophers, mystics, teachers, and spiritual scholars understood the relationship between thought, emotion, consciousness, and reality. They understood that the mind is creative, that belief shapes experience, and that life responds to awareness.

The first book, **Profound**, is about remembering. It is about gathering ancient wisdom and recognizing truths that may feel familiar even if you are encountering them for the first time. This is the awakening stage. The moment when something inside you says, "There is more."

The second book, **Activate**, is about embodiment. Knowledge alone does not change a life. It must be practiced. This book moves wisdom from the intellect into daily living. It teaches you how to tap into the divine energy within you and apply what you have learned in practical, grounded ways.

The third book, **Think**, is about mastery of the mind. Thought is not passive. It is creative. This book guides you in becoming aware of your inner dialogue, understanding how thoughts shape experience, and learning how to consciously direct the mental patterns that influence your life.

The fourth book, **Live**, is about integration. This is where knowledge, practice, and awareness become who you are. You no longer strive to be aligned. You live aligned. You move through the world with clarity, compassion, and confidence, embodying the wisdom you have gained.

Together, these four books form a complete journey.

Awakening. Activation. Mastery. Expression.

This is not a quick fix. It is not spiritual bypassing. It is not about perfection. It is about responsibility. Responsibility for your thoughts. Responsibility for your emotional state. Responsibility for the energy you bring into the world.

The world does not need more information. It needs more

conscious people. People who are self-aware. People who understand cause and effect at the level of thought and emotion. People who can pause, reflect, and respond instead of react. People who live from inner alignment rather than fear.

You were never meant to live small, disconnected, or powerless. You were meant to participate in your own evolution.

This series is an invitation. Not to abandon what you believe, but to expand it. Not to follow me, but to follow your own inner knowing. Not to search endlessly outside yourself, but to reconnect with what has always been within you.

If you are reading this, you are ready.

Ready to remember.

Ready to activate.

Ready to master your mind.

Ready to live fully.

Welcome to the journey.

Dating after 50

Dating after 50 is not for the faint of heart, but it *can* be healing, hilarious, and empowering.

Over 50 and Still Fine is an honest, relatable, and uplifting guide for anyone stepping back into the dating world after heartbreak, divorce, long-term relationships, or years of choosing themselves first. With humor and raw transparency, SaBrina Fisher Reece shares real stories, lessons learned, and the emotional growth that comes with midlife dating.

This book is not about pretending dating is easy, it's about navigating the awkward moments, the red flags, the hope, the disappointment, and the unexpected joy with wisdom and self-respect. SaBrina reminds readers that healing doesn't mean shutting down, and confidence doesn't come from being chosen, it comes from knowing your worth.

Inside, you'll laugh, reflect, and recognize yourself as you explore:

Dating with boundaries instead of desperation

Healing old wounds while opening your heart again

Recognizing patterns and avoiding emotional burnout

Choosing peace, clarity, and self-love at every stage

If you're over 50, still fine, and considering love again, this book is your reminder that your story isn't over, your heart isn't broken beyond repair, and it's never too late to date with intention, humor, and confidence.

www.ingramcontent.com/pod-product-compliance
Lightning Source LLC
Chambersburg PA
CBHW070855050426
42453CB00012B/2220